CW01034458

The Women's Peac
1917 – 1918

Crusading Women in Manchester and East Lancashire

The 'Real Rebels' of WW1

Anti-militarist, socialist and internationalist

First published 2017

Manchester Metropolitan University

All Saints, Manchester M15 6BH

© Manchester Metropolitan University

A catalogue record of this book is available from the British Library

ISBN 978-1-910029-27-5

Printed by Manchester Metropolitan University

Chapter	Page

Preface by *Dr. Alison Ronan*

Crusading women; an academic/volunteer co-production research funded by AHRC Voices of War and Peace

The Women's Peace Crusade swept though industrial East Lancashire in the summer of 1917. It was part of a series of spontaneous women-led demonstrations across the country, mobilised by socialist and internationalist women, urging the Government to negotiate a peace.

This specific piece of research aimed to uncover the ordinary Crusader, the local and 'unheard' women in the cotton spinning and weaving towns of Blackburn, Manchester, Burnley and Nelson, Oldham, Rochdale and Bolton, towns where recruiting was strong. We have also had contributions from researchers in Bradford and Cumbria.

The research has been led by a team of dedicated and enthusiastic volunteers working alongside archivists in local archives. Academic Dr. Alison Ronan coordinated the research, working with support from the Centre for Regional History in Manchester Metropolitan University. The volunteers have met regularly to compare their research and findings and Dr. Alison Ronan has gone to visit each small team in their archives, working together with the researchers.

The newly recovered stories form the basis of the film made by the Clapham Film Unit and scripted by Hazel Roy. The film recreated the Crusades in East Lancashire, using the fictional cycle journey of the young Manchester undergraduate and Women's International League member, Mabel Phythian, to link up the Crusades from Manchester to Nelson.

Most of these local stories have not been told in any detail before: the research has used material from newspapers of the time, the directory of Crusade organisers and their addresses, published in the *Labour Leader* in the summer of 1917, census returns and local lists of Conscientious Objectors taken from the Cyril Pearce Register (IWM). Some of the material has changed our understanding of the Crusade locally and has revealed many previously unknown local women who were coordinating local demonstrations.These 'ordinary' women have truly been hidden from history.

This book fleshes out some of the stories, writing up biographies of many local women and telling many more of the narratives which have been uncovered. It looks at the newly recovered stories from the textile towns of East Lancashire, each town having a dedicated chapter, some written by the volunteers but each drawing on the material that has come to light in the research. Dedicated space is given to radical women from each town.

We hope you enjoy this book as much as we have enjoyed writing it.

For more details of the research please go to

http://www.pixnet.co.uk/Oldham-hrg/World-War1/Menu.html.

Making the Book: *Dr. Alison Ronan*

Be astonished by the detailed accounts of a riot in **Oldham**! Find out how **Manchester** was silenced! See how links were made in **Rochdale** with other campaigns for peace! Find out why **Manchester** women were imprisoned in the summer of 1917. Read new stories of the indefatigable **Women's Co-operative Guild**. See what happened in **Cumbria** when an activist, sacked from teaching, takes on the organising of local Crusades. See why more women were imprisoned in **Bradford** and what happened in **Bolton**, where the Crusade went largely unreported by the local press. In **Blackburn** and **Nelson**, conscientious objector families, local socialist weavers and suffragists came out in their thousands to support the Crusades. Read about the radical women in each town who organised and supported the Crusades.

Although I have edited the book, and added some factual information, each chapter retains the individual characteristics of the author[s]. There is a short piece by an actor, the film maker and script writer and a copy of the entire film script, which was edited in the final film version.

The project also wanted to write about the enduring campaigns against militarism and war: so we have included a piece which links contemporary international, national and local campaigns for peace. As the Greenham Common women sang:

'You can't kill the spirit, she's like a mountain / old and strong, she goes on and on.'

Emma Thomas on playing Lydia Leach – the 'fancy' weaver from Blackburn

When I first saw they were looking for an actress to play the part of Lydia Leach *"speaking with passion and a Blackburn accent about the wrongs being done to young men who had been conscripted and the women left to fend for families"*, I knew straight away this part was for me. Being very passionate and extremely opinionated on the wrongs being done in the world today, I felt I could give this woman from history a truth and relevance to the present day.

I was brought up by a working class woman. Brought up single handedly by my mother, a born fighter, a born lefty! Having been through struggles of my own – frequently relocating as a youth, money troubles, bad relationships and of course being a woman, I was destined for a role like this.

My mother has made me into the woman I am today and without strong, brave women like Lydia Leach we would not have the voice we have today. I have such respect and adulation for the fighting and hard work done by these women to get us the vote, to let us be heard.

All these inspiring women have been hidden throughout history, stored away in dusty places to be forgotten, no awards, no recognition – until now. To be part of an independent English film and help these women to finally get the acknowledgement they deserve is very humbling, and more important than ever.

The recent rise of the far right across the Western World and the wave of prejudice that has come with it means we need people to fight, and if Lydia and I have one thing in common it's that we will fight; we will stand!

People used to laugh at the thought of women getting the vote: well, let them laugh again.

We will make a difference!

Filming in Blackburn September 30 2016

The Women's Peace Crusade by *Dr. Alison Ronan*

Barrow to Bristol,
Manchester to Melksham,
Accrington to Aberdeen,
Nelson to Norwich... ... ...

The socialist, feminist and internationalist Women's Peace Crusade ran like a whirlwind across the country during 1917 and 1918.

By the end of the war, there had been 123 Crusades in all the industrial towns across England, Scotland, Wales and Ireland. The Crusade paved the way for women's peace activism over the next 100 years, as one of the researchers/contributors remembered from her own activism:

British Casualties for Week Ending July 21.

Officers, Killed	201
Men, Killed	4,881
Officers, Wounded and Missing ...	472
Men, Wounded and Missing	13,504
	19,058

'Labour Leader' July 1917

On Saturday 27 October 1984, I 'died' in Barrow-in-Furness. I had travelled from London alongside many other women and men to a protest called by the Campaign for Nuclear Disarmament against Trident nuclear missiles. Once there we marched together until, at a predetermined time, we 'died' by lying down in the streets and refusing to move. Ship building Barrow was the focus – as it was where the 'Trident Dock' was located.

In 1916, ship-building Glasgow, known as Red Clydeside, had been the crucible of the Women's Peace Crusade. It erupted there in the summer of the Somme, where women speakers, demanding a negotiated peace, attracted a huge crowd on Glasgow Green. Speakers came from across the country and from a variety of feminist and women's rights campaigns. These women were equally concerned about women's working condition, high food prices, profiteering, sugar rationing and unjust taxes as well as continuing the struggle for suffrage, fair divorce laws and improved infant and maternal health.

The determined pacifist and Women's International League campaigner, Margaret Ashton from Manchester, was the headline speaker, already a seasoned suffrage and women's rights campaigner, she was now a resolute supporter of the Crusade.

The strategies of mobilising local women, having meetings that coincided with shifts at the factories and the mills and canvassing door-to-door in working class neighbourhoods, became important features of the Crusade as it gathered pace across the country again in 1917 after the first Russian Revolution.

Women campaigners organised street meetings in working class areas of the city and ran public meetings at times best suited to the participation of working class women. The Crusade deliberately targeted working class women, canvassing door to door in the inner city streets around the mills and factories, often using the language of housework to drive home their political message-asking *Shall we not speak for ourselves? Shall we remain silent any longer?' (Forward* July 22 1916)

The Crusade in textile Lancashire

This project is a story about local women in the textile towns of East Lancashire who were prepared to get out on the streets of their local

Clarion Cycling Club, Salford 1912 (Working Class Movement Library)

towns in 1917 to demand that the Government start peace negotiations. These were women politicised by war who were prepared to risk arrest by handing out handbills that contravened the draconian Defence of the Realm Act – at least 3 of them were imprisoned-prepared for threats and ridicule-but still prepared to be part of the Women's Peace Crusade.

This is a story about local working class women: women who were sick of the slaughter, sick of having no coal, no food and sick of war. By 1917, the war was in its third year, disrupting family life and bringing death, hunger and uncertainty into cities and towns across the country. It also threatened individual freedom with the introduction of military conscription in February 1916 while the Defence of the Realm Act made the publication or distribution of any pro-peace or anti-war literature very difficult. There was constant, simmering industrial unrest as the Ministry of Munitions controlled more and more factories and engineering works.

The towns in East Lancashire were industrial centres built on cotton and weaving, with strong trade unions and solid socialist and co-operative traditions. In Nelson particularly, there was a lively Independent Labour Party with its own Socialist Institution and Sunday school. People here were used to protesting about wages, the suffrage and the iniquities of capitalism. In the immediate years before the war, working class women in East Lancashire had been involved in the Election Fighting Fund, an alliance between the non-militant suffragists and the Labour Party to encourage the election of pro-suffrage men to parliament-and so-the necessary networks were already in place for women to mobilise during the war.

Nelson Socialist Institution: and stained glass window c. 1916. Drawing by Emily Johns 2016.

For many local socialists and pacifists, the first Russian revolution in early 1917 was a significant event, opening up the possibilities of a *People's Peace*, an opportunity for transparent diplomacy and different ways of government. As Margaret Ashton declared:

> *The Russian revolution had opened up the possibility of government by consent and free will of the people, taking the place of government by authority.*

There was hope in the air.

The Women's Peace Crusade was a grass-root, feminist, anti-militarist and socialist campaign. Thousands of women took to the streets in towns across the country, demanding a negotiated and just peace. Children and young women from the local Socialist Sunday Schools swelled the Crusades. There were badges depicting the Angel of Peace and leaflets handed out. Choirs sang. The Crusades attracted crowds of over 2000 or 3000 women and children, peacefully marching but banging dustbin lids, waving banners and football rattles, singing hymns and handing out pacifist material. Often they were heckled, threatened and their demonstrations broken up. By the summer of 1917, more than a million leaflets donated by the Labour Press and the ILP, along with Peace 'buttons', had been distributed throughout the country. But by the winter of 1917, new regulations under the Defence of the Realm Act meant that many of the WPC leaflets were seized and it became illegal to print or distribute leaflets on the subjects of war and peace.

Original 1917 WPC 'button' (with thanks to Dr Christopher Bailey)

The Crusade was organised by an ad-hoc committee of socialist women led by socialist Ethel Snowden. From June 1917, she wrote a Crusade column in the *Labour Leader* which was edited by her fellow socialist Katherine Bruce Glasier (Fenner Brockway, the previous editor, was in prison as a conscientious objector). The *Leader* also published the numbers of casualties each week from 1917. The numbers are truly unbearable, 23,000 in one week alone, in August 1917, during the battle of Passendale.

The Crusade made clear the links between militarism and the arms trade, businesses profiteering from the war, the lack of coal and food. It brought a political and socialist perspective to the fore.

A key tactic of the campaigns for the vote had been to 'make more noise'. That meant standing up at public meetings, in music halls and theatres, scrawling 'votes for women' over census papers, demonstrating on the streets and disrupting elections. The Glasgow Rent strikes, which preceded the Crusade, but which greatly influenced its strategies, had used the tactics of banging steel dustbin lids on the streets and marching through the streets with placards and homemade banners. Well-known political women spoke at Crusades across the country: Sylvia Pankhurst spoke at numerous Crusades in Lancashire, Cllr. Margaret Ashton from Manchester, Charlotte Despard (founder of the Women's Freedom League in 1907) Eva Gore Booth (sister of Sinn Fein's Countess Markievicz) and her companion Esther Roper, devoted most of their activism in 1917/1918 to supporting the Crusade. What is astonishing is the complex network of activists and speakers who were prepared to travel, crisscrossing the country, to demand that the Government listen to the unheard voices of 'reason and humanity' and the Women's Peace Crusade. These are the stories of a few of those Crusades and the 'ordinary' women who organised them in East Lancashire.

Drawing by Emily Johns 2016

Manchester was a radical, cosmopolitan, non-conformist, industrial city, built on cotton and engineering. It was the cradle of the Votes for Women campaign. There was a strong tradition of social reform and radical politics. Although recruiting was strong in Manchester there was a lively anti-war movement involving socialists, suffragists, Quakers and the No-Conscription Fellowship which was established here.

Burnley was known as "The Largest Producer of Woven Cotton Cloth in the World" because of its geographical position and the opening of the Leeds & Liverpool Canal in 1816 but, by 1914, the town was suffering from a massive slump in its textile industry. Over four thousand men in Burnley were killed in the war and many more enlisted.

Nelson was a 'radical' new town and its Weavers' Association was known as the most militant textile union. By 1914 the town was a hotbed of people holding anti-militarist and socialist views. Peace meetings were well attended and Nelson was said to have one of the highest numbers of conscientious objectors in the country.

Bolton has a textile tradition going back to the 14th century. During the 19th-century it was an important centre for cotton spinning and also for numerous associated bleach and dye works. In addition, the coming of the railways saw the establishment of a large locomotive works at nearby Horwich. In the 1930s, it was the location for the first Mass Observation exercise, conducted by self-taught anthropologist Tom Harrisson, who gave it the pseudonym 'Worktown'.

Oldham was a cotton spinning town, which, at its peak at the start of the 20th century, had more than 10% of the world's spindles. Machinery manufacturers exported around the world and skilled foundry men became important in providing munitions during WW1. Over 90 men from Oldham were Conscientious Objectors and in 1918, one of them, William Edward Burns, died whilst being force fed in Hull Jail.

Blackburn was an industrialised cotton spinning and weaving town with a pacifist Labour MP Philip Snowden. His wife, Ethel Snowden, co-ordinated the Peace Crusade.

Rochdale had been a weaving town since the 16th century and by the early 20th century, spinning and weaving were the main industries. It was the birthplace of the modern Co-operative Movement with the Rochdale pioneers opening their first shop on Toad Lane in 1844.

Toad Lane, Rochdale

Abbreviations

CO	Conscientious Objector
DORA	Defence of the Realm Act
FoR	Fellowship of Reconciliation
ILP	Independent Labour Party
NCF	No-Conscription Fellowship
NUWSS	National Union of Women's Suffrage Societies
UDC	Union of Democratic Control
US	United Suffragists
WCG	Women's Co-operative Guild
WFL	Women's Freedom League
WIL	Women's International League
WPC	Women's Peace Crusade
WSPU	Women's Social and Political Union

Main anti-war groups in WW1

1. The **Union of Democratic Control**, established during the first few days of the war by Liberal and Labour politicians, argued for a clearer and more transparent parliamentary control of foreign policy and a just peace settlement. It was one of the first political groups to involve women at all levels of the organisation.

2. The **Fellowship of Reconciliation**: The Fellowship was established in England in the winter 1914 and worked closely with the No-Conscription Fellowship. It was against all war. It is still in existence.

3. The **No-Conscription Fellowship** was formed in 1914 to support men who were not prepared to fight. It had branches across the country.

4. The **Women's International League** was established after the Women's International Congress in The Hague in 1915. The League was committed to civil liberties, a just peace, education for peace and argued for votes for all, rather than a limited suffrage. It is still in existence

5. The **Independent Labour Party**: Many local people were drawn to the ILP during the war because of its anti-war, anti-militarist, socialist approach.

6. The **United Suffragists**: absorbed women in a revitalised suffrage campaign, after the Speakers conference in 1915 met to redraw the limits of the franchise. Lillian Williamson Forrester, the young militant Manchester suffragette, imprisoned for her role in the attack on Manchester Art Gallery in 1913, declared in 1916 (somewhat paradoxically) that *'The great duty of suffrage women is to speak peace.'*

WPC handbill (John Rylands Library)

Manchester Silenced! *by Dr. Alison Ronan.*

On 10 July 1917, in city-centre Manchester, a hundred local women crowded into a small downstairs room in the socialist Clarion Café on Market Street. They were planning a local anti-war demonstration as part of the Women's Peace Crusade. The meeting had been convened by women from the local branch of the anti-militarist Independent Labour Party drawing on their contacts with other women who were opposed to the war. Young socialist Agnes Whittaker from Longsight was the local WPC secretary.

There was a large and receptive audience for the WPC demonstration held on July 22nd 1917, in the traditional city-centre meeting site of Stevenson Square, just off Piccadilly Gardens. The Crusade was chaired by socialist Annot Robinson and the speakers on the platform included The Hon. Lady Barlow a local Quaker, who had signed the Open letter to German and Austrian women in the winter 1914/5, she spoke alongside Charlotte Despard, well-known suffragist and speaker for the WPC. Councillor Margaret Ashton was another speaker, who will have been well known locally from her position as a local councillor and her commitment to suffrage, women's rights and peace. Katherine Bruce Glasier was another speaker and, as one of the organizing committee for the Women's Peace Crusade, her attendance on the platform of the first Manchester campaign showed

Stevenson Square c.1915

solidarity, support and friendship. Suffragist Elizabeth Muter Wilson was another speaker. She had been involved in the pre-war suffrage movement in Manchester and was a regular speaker on the suffrage circuit and for the Women's International League.

Another speaker was Mrs. Hannah Mitchell, a committed socialist and anti-conscriptionist. Agatha Watts was another speaker. She was a committed Quaker, a pacifist and suffragist, part of the WIL and may have attracted local women from her neighbourhood of Longsight and from her Quaker networks. The final speaker, trade unionist Emily Cox, had been involved in the pre-war suffrage campaigns and was a member of the Women's Trade Union Council.

The *Labour Leader* reported that the meeting in the Square on July 22 raised £7 13s 3d and the Manchester branch had raised £14 4s 9p. Another meeting for all women was advertised in the *Labour Leader* to be held in the Clarion Café on Monday 23 July

OTHER MEETINGS.

A WOMEN'S PEACE MEETING will be held in STEVENSON SQUARE, ON SATURDAY, SEPTEMBER 8, at 3 p.m. Speakers: Mrs. PHILIP SNOWDEN. Mrs. BARTON (Sheffield). Miss MARGARET ASHTON.

'Labour Leader' September 1917

1917. This was to plan the next 'demonstration' in Platt Fields although eventually it was planned for Stevenson Square again, on September 8 1917. Ethel Snowden, one of the Crusade's organizing committee, was to speak, also Margaret Ashton and a representative from the Women's Co-operative Guild, Mrs. Eleanor Barton from Sheffield. The meeting was to advocate the immediate opening of negotiations for peace, and a *Manchester Guardian* article on September 10th 1917 mentions Katherine Bruce Glasier and Mrs. Smith from the International Women's Peace association, as additional speakers.

But the meeting was stopped by the police who had, according to the *Manchester Guardian* on 10th September 1917: *'Anticipated that attempts would be made by opponents of a peace policy, to interfere with the meeting, or to hold a counter demonstration.'*

Margaret Ashton, writing a letter to the same edition, very much regrets this action and emphasises that the Women's Peace Crusade is neither pro-German nor unpatriotic. She cites *'tremendous majorities at open meetings in Leeds, York, Birmingham, Glasgow, Blackburn, Nelson and other towns'*.

But there was discontent in the air… on 6 July 1917, just before the first Crusade, the *Manchester Guardian* reported that the Commission for the North West on Industrial Unrest had visited the Manchester and Salford ILP to discuss the unrest caused by the high cost of living and the lack of a coherent rationing policy. The *Labour Leader* reports that the police raided a meeting organised in Manchester to celebrate the *'dawn of freedom in Russia'*. The Manchester campaign collapsed but the women continued to support other Crusades across the NW and their names crop up time and time again throughout these pages tracking the Peace Crusade across Lancashire, Yorkshire, Cumberland and Westmorland during 1917-1918.

But women were always creative as young activist Mabel Phythian recalled in November 1917, *'I remember being in the Women's International League office – looking across to Manchester Town Hall, and on one occasion I was in the office for some reason, and the police raided it. We had some pamphlets which were banned-I knew the Salford police didn't ban and the Manchester police did ban the lists of casualties. And we had great fun just going over the Manchester boundary and handing out the lists to Manchester people crossing the Salford boundary!'* (Quoted in Liddington *The Long Road to Greenham*) There were no more Crusades in Manchester after 1917 but peace meetings continued in the city until the end of the war.

These two Manchester women, ardent socialists and members of the local No-Conscription Fellowship, arrived at the Prees Heath army training camp near Whitchurch, Shropshire, in July 1917. Their aim was simple: to distribute anti-war literature to local people and the soldiers at the camp. Maud Hayes was a young widow, her husband John had died earlier in the year, although they were already estranged. Phillis Skinner's husband, 27 year old conscientious objector Allen, was in Wormwood Scrubs serving 2 years with hard labour. Her son Jack aged 2, was staying with friends.

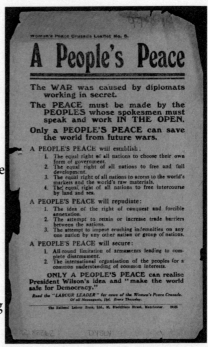

WPC handbill (John Rylands Library)

Emma Jones, from Whitchurch, had written sympathetically to the Manchester women, as Phillis had been to Prees Heath earlier that year to attend Allen's court martial, and was now coming to Shropshire 'en route' to London to see Allen in Wormwood Scrubs. The women were driven to the training camp in Emma Jones' donkey cart. Emma was another socialist: she had written to Phillis in June 1917 – *'Today is to be a great day in Leeds- the Independent Labour Party convention. I am glad we have among us brave men who will not bow their knee to the god of war. The day will come when the people of*

England will not allow injustice to continue'. The three women were arrested near Market Drayton at 10pm by a local policeman and after a trial Phillis and Maud were imprisoned and Emma Jones fined £2. Transcripts of the trial suggest that Phillis tried to take most of the blame and indeed she was imprisoned for a longer time than Maud. Phillis was used to controversy: her first husband had divorced her in 1912 when she had run away from London to live with Allen Skinner, lying consistently about her age – telling the police in Whitchurch that she was 35 when she was 43!

Both Phillis and Maud were involved in the No-Conscription Fellowship in Manchester and in 1918 the local CO journal recorded that *'Not often do we hear of our COs walking from the prison to the altar. But such a thing happened on Tuesday July 22. Mr [Edwin] Rodway who was discharged from Winchester prison on June 28 celebrated his release in a most tangible manner by taking' unto himself a wife'.* The happy bride, Mrs Hayes, being herself a staunch CO [and]it is of interest to know that she also has done term in the 'mansion of the Blest' just twelve months ago'.

Maud and Edwin stayed in Manchester after the war. Nothing more is known about them.

Phillis and Allen moved to London in 1920. Allen had been released from prison in 1918 on the grounds of ill health. Allen was always involved in the anti-war movement and he edited *Peace News* during the 50s. Phillis died in 1950, Allen in 1974. Their son Jack was a CO in WW2.

The Oldham Riot! *August 6th 1917: by Dr. Alison Ronan*

Research by Sheila Goodyear and Dorothy Bintley.
(Photos from Oldham Local Studies and Archive)

Town Hall Oldham c 1914

In July 1916 several Oldham men appealed to the Oldham Tribunal for exemption from service on the ground that they held a conscientious objection to war and were against having any connection with war. Over 90 COs have been discovered in Oldham and suburbs. And by 1917, a war-weary Oldham must have wanted peace more than anything. There was to be a peace week in Oldham and it was clear that the ILP and the Women's International League and the No-Conscription Fellowship were working closely together. This was the planned peace "mission" for August 1917:

Monday 6th, at 7:30, at the Market Place, J.W. Moor from Rochdale ILP; Tuesday, at 7:30 at the Park Gates, R.C. Wallhead [a well-known ILP

activist from Manchester]
Wednesday, at 7:30 at Barry Street, J.W. Moor;
Thursday, at 7:30 at the Park Gates, the [formidable suffragist] Manchester
Councillor Margaret Ashton;
Friday at 7:30, at the Market Place, R.C. Wallhead;
Saturday 11th at 7:30, at the Park Gates, [Manchester Quaker] Mrs. Watts.
[Ed: words in brackets added]

But the rally on August 6th collapsed – as the headline in next day's
Oldham Standard, declared,

THE PEACEITES(sic) Complete Rout in Oldham Meeting Abandoned
WHITE FEATHER CREW TAKE REFUGE IN TOWN HALL and
I.L.P. ROOMS LOOTED

Conspicuous amongst the crowd on August 6th had been a large group
of soldiers, from a New Zealand Field Artillery Battery, who were

High street, Oldham c 1914

quartered at Chadderton Camp. Also in the crowd were a number of policemen, some of whom were in uniform and others in plain clothes.

The crowd continued to grow; heckling and jeering increased even though '... *one of the peace missionaries tried to say that his three sons were fighting but few heard and it made no impression.*' As they reached the Town Hall '... *all at once an attack was made on Mr. Hill [secretary of the ILP]. Down he went on the setts. Up he was pulled, and battered, struck by anyone who could get near enough*'. The police intervened and at this point it could have appeared that peace and order might return to the streets but some young women (perhaps local peace activists Elsie Winterbottom and young teacher Miss Quarmby) were heard to voice their opinion, '... *of the way in which the brutal crowd had dealt with their friends*'.

Their friends included Arthur Winterbottom, Elsie's brother, who was a bank Clerk from Chamber Road, and a conscientious objector. Arthur nearly reached St. Patrick's Church, when several of the New Zealand soldiers made a grab for him. He '... *was frogmarched back again, shouting for mercy. He was badly maltreated*'. The hostile crowd then marched to the I.L.P rooms which were ransacked and anything loose, including leaflets, books, flags and even curtains were thrown out of the windows into the crowd below.

A hostile editorial in the Saturday edition of the '*Standard*' was headlined,

'DISAPPOINTED CROWD AT PARK GATE'
'*The Peacemongers of Oldham, who so ostentatiously advertised a weeks' mission in the borough, had such a tremendous drubbing on the first night that the remainder of the programme was unceremoniously cancelled. ... So ignominiously ends a most impudent attempt on the part of a handful of cranks to push their pernicious nostrums on a patriotic people.*'

During the week when there should have been the series of Peace Meetings, letters on the subject were sent to the *'Chronicle'* and a selection was printed. Most of these letters focused on the desire for peace but, *'not one at any price'*. One letter expresses the hope that, *'we all want peace but it must be for good, not so that the enemy can start again when our children are grown to be men.'*

Across the town there were a number of individual conscientious objectors, Quakers, I.L.P. men and women and other organisations like the No-Conscription Fellowship and Women's International League working for a negotiated peace but there appears to have been very little general support across the borough. Those who chose to publicly support this cause would pay a heavy price. One letter to the paper chose to remain anonymous, signing off as an I.L.P.er, *'In view of the present government by a jingo press and the acceptance of the law of the mob, for the safety of my wife and children, I must withhold my name.'*

The end result was that no more peace meetings appear to have been held in Oldham.

Henshaw Street, Oldham c1917

'Those outspoken women':
Elsie Winterbottom, Miss Quarmby and the Peace rallies in Oldham

By 1917 the Women's International League [WIL] in the North West had been loosely superimposed on the pre-war suffragist branch network. The Manchester branch of the League had over 500 members. The League had grown out of the International Congress of Women in The Hague in 1915, which was committed to peace and demanding that women had a voice in public affairs.

Both young Elsie Winterbottom, a secretary and local teacher Miss Quarmby were the secretaries of Oldham's Women's International League in 1916 and 1917 respectively and because there was an *absolute connection* between the WIL and the Votes for Women campaign we can imagine that both Miss Winterbottom and Miss Quarmby were also suffragists – non-party and non-militant.

By 1917, the Women's International League was also working closely with local branches of the No-Conscription Fellowship and the Independent Labour Party to mobilise women for the Women's Peace Crusade.

Elsie's brother Arthur was a conscientious objector, a 26 year old bank clerk, newly married to Alice Taylor, a local school teacher. He asked for absolute exemption from military service because he *'believed all war to be wrong and contrary to the highest and moral instincts of humanity... force was no remedy for evil' (Oldham Evening Chronicle* July 4 1916)

When Arthur and his ILP colleagues were badly beaten up during the start of the Peace Mission on August 6th 1917 some young women were heard to voice their opinion, this was no doubt Elsie and Miss Quarmby. They complained '... *of the way in which the brutal crowd had dealt with their friends., "like lions and tigers, my love," and how they had the right to free speech* ...' It certainly incensed the crowd who then ransacked the ILP rooms.

Arthur did not stay in the bank. He was unfit for active service (from other evidence it seems that he had a slight disability in one arm), Oldham Tribunal exempted him from combatant service but not from non-combatant service. He was told to seek work of national importance as a clerk with the railway or canal company. It was standard for men sent for Work of National Importance to be given two weeks to find work – it was their responsibility not the Tribunal's. Oldham had an approved list including work in market gardens and small holdings. It seems likely that Arthur took on work on the land during the war as, at some stage, he and his wife, sister and mother all moved to Congleton where they set up a market garden. His son was born in 1920 in Congleton.

Miss Quarmby was sacked from her post at Oldham High School in 1918 and no more is known about her.

The Women's Co-operative Guild in the NW in WW1: by Jane Ward and Angela Downing.

Members of the Women's Co-operative Guild [WCG] were a formidable band of campaigners for peace, justice and social reforms throughout the First World War.

The Guild used the Women's Corner section of the national paper *Co-operative News* as a space to campaign for peace and debate big questions of the time. Margaret Llewelyn Davies became the first general secretary and devoted her life to the WCG believing that, *'it is an ideal instrument for carrying to working class housewives the message for the emancipation of women'*.

(Working Class Movement Library)

North West women were very active locally and nationally. Trade union activist, suffragist and pacifist Sarah Reddish, from Bolton, became the first paid Guild organiser.

The Guild was very active throughout the war. Margaret Llewelyn Davies was a pacifist. Locally members' lives changed hugely as they entered the workforce in greater numbers than ever before, suffered the terrible deaths and injuries of male family members, the persecution of conscientious objectors and struggled to feed their families in the face of food shortages and high prices.

(Image courtesy of the National Co-operative Archive)

The women became resolute campaigners, railing against the war, women's working conditions, high food prices, profiteering, sugar rationing and unjust taxes as well as continuing the struggle for suffrage, fair divorce laws and improved infant and maternal health. Like the wider Co-operative movement, the Guild was generally pro-peace although the views of individual members differed and some members resigned because of this. Mrs Scott, a 'felt hat worker' from Stockport, noted that during the War her branch of the Guild '*had kept firm opposition to the war, and worked for peace. Our membership dropped from 100 to 20 or 30.*' The war was debated in the Women's Corner letters pages, often linked to the values of cooperation and urging women to become peacemakers. Most WCG women were against conscription, Mrs. A.E. Branmere of 16, Central Rd, Gorton, sent this motion from their branch meeting "*that we, members of the Droylsden Women's Guild protest against the institution of Conscription or compulsion as indicated by the Conscription Bill, which has passed its second reading in the House of Commons, believing that compulsion is contrary to our national traditions, inimical to the best interests of the Workers and subversive of all true progress and liberty*"

The branch most strongly against conscription was Huddersfield where there was a lively No-Conscription Fellowship branch and many men were COs.

In the war years, women entered employment outside the home in larger numbers than ever before, often working in highly exploitative and unsafe toxic conditions for lower pay than their male counterparts. Co-operative women started to campaign with male trade unionists for women workers' rights at work as well as setting up schemes to help poor working women. In January 1915 Mary Quaile, local trade union and No-Conscription Fellowship activist, spoke to the Eccles Guild about worker exploitation in the interests of large profits, urging women to join trades unions to protect their rights. The Women's

Corner reported an interview that trade union activist Mary Macarthur gave to the *Daily News,* protesting against the low wages paid to women working in controlled establishments which they were unable to leave without permission of the employer or the local tribunal. In 1917 the Women's Corner reported the shocking case of fines levied on women for refusing to work with CE, a powder used in shell filling factories that ruined their health. Local socialist and pacifist Annot Robinson spoke to the Swinton branch highlighting the disparity of wages in the munitions industries: both Robinson and Quaile were involved in the local Women's War Interest Committee, arguing for equality of pay and working conditions.

By 1917 co-operative women's demands for a negotiated and just peace became more and more international in outlook and with the wider Cooperative movement, they turned their attention to post war

'Co-operative News' 1916; Nelson WCG
(Image courtesy of the National Co-operative Archive)

planning with a strong international emphasis. At the 1917 Congress there was a resolution to support the Russian appeal for peace without conquest: *'We trust that social reforms in foreshadowed will build up a Co-operative State in Russia which will lay the foundations for the international co-operation essential to world-wide peace.*

Women also debated their vision of post-war society. An editorial in June 1917 asked *'Which is it to be? Are we to be more pacifist or more militarist? Let the mothers take the lead'*, and pleads for a more pacifist nation after the war, insisting that: *'their children being taught to respect the freedom and the*  *rights of other countries and to recognise in the worker of other countries fellow workers of their own. If this is the spirit of teaching but only so we may hope that the next generation will find the way to seek peace and ensure it.'*

The issue of suffrage and the war was constantly referred to by the Guildswomen. Writing in Women's Corner, Elizabeth from Loughborough urged all women to use the vote, once women have it, to stop war. A sentiment echoed by Eccles activist Alice Nevitt. The vote, peace and economics were the very stuff of this feminist co-operative activism.

(Image courtesy of the National Co-operative Archive)

The Women's Co-operative Guild and Direct Action!

'We have been holding our protest meetings, our conferences and our talky talky meetings. We have made impassioned speeches, we have protested with all our vigour. Meanwhile prices have soared. We have effected nothing. The women of Maryport did not bother with holding meetings; they took action and forced prices down with a rush.'
Co-operative News Women's Corner 1917

Co-operative women agitated against high prices and food shortages throughout the war. Women from Maryport in Cumbria even resorted to direct action.

They organised a boycott of geese at the 1916 Christmas market that reduced the price from 1s 3d per lb to 9d per lb. They were in action again at the market in 1917, remonstrating with farmers who were asking double the government fixed price of one shilling a stone for potatoes. When their protests were ignored the women threw carrots and turnips until they were able to buy for the shilling. A farmer

(Image courtesy of the National Co-operative Archive)

who complained that he could not get labour to dig his potatoes, provoked a massed attack on his fields to *'rescue the potatoes from decay and themselves from hunger'*. There was admiration in the movement but also some disapproval for this militancy. The Women's Corner editor acknowledged the anger of people who were finding difficulties obtaining food but would be sorry to see the Cumberland method applied generally.

Other local WCG activists included Mrs. Yearn from Oldham who was an early trade unionist, and persuaded all the other women in the mill to join the union and was promptly sacked. She then joined the Women's Co-operative Guild and attended Congress in Liverpool in 1915, which she said made her *"a real rebel"* and declared that, *'I have worked wholeheartedly for a better existence"*.

Eccles activist Mrs. Alice Nevitt moved through the ranks of the local WCG, and became much more visible in national Co-op business. In 1917 she declared, *'There had been 20,000,000 casualties up to now, and that meant that millions of mothers had made great sacrifices. The individual feeling of revenge must be put on one side, and the idea must be peace for the good of the whole community'*. This call for peace without conquest was very controversial.

At a meeting of 300 WCG women from the Lancashire region held in Holyoake House in 1917, Mrs. Nevitt reminded women to continue campaigning for the vote for all women. She also says that as this is the first time that they have met together since the Russian Revolution, that the meeting should send congratulations to the co-operators who had *"thrown off the chains of despotism"*. In 1918 Mrs. Nevitt reminded members of the Eccles branch that during the war they had campaigned against *'unfairness in food distribution, taxes on excess profits'*, and *'unfairness in tribunals'* and now urged women who have the Vote, to become involved in politics.

Image courtesy of Dr Christopher Bailey

Untold tales of the Crusade in Bolton: *by Barry Mills, Margaret Koppens and Lois Dean.*

The scant reporting of the Peace Crusade in Bolton seems to imply that the Crusade never really took off in the town but there were plenty of local suffragists, internationalist women and a number of conscientious objectors whose families would have supported the Crusade. Although never as politically radical as some of its Lancashire neighbours, the town could lay claim to some of those who fought for the cause of peace, rather than war. Reverend Sir Herbert Dunnico MP (1875-1953), became involved with Peace Society and was its secretary in 1916 forming the *Peace Negotiation Committee* to call for a truce with Germany. His brother was a conscientious objector.

Bolton newspapers were very reluctant to report on any opposition to the war and consequently there are few references to the Bolton branch of the Women's Peace Crusade in the town's archives, nor in the local newspapers.

When the Government formally introduced Censorship in 1917, the *Bolton Chronicle* commented that this measure was unnecessary because the local newspapers were so **responsible** – in other words their self-censorship was already complete. The situation was different in towns such as Blackburn and Burnley, where the newspapers were equally pro-war but were unable to ignore the views of their local MPs – Philip Snowden in Blackburn tirelessly working in

Drawing by Emily Johns 2016

support of individual COs and MP Philip Morrell at Burnley raising questions about ill treatment of COs in Parliament. In addition, Philip Snowden's wife, Ethel, became such a well-known political figure that the local papers could not ignore her. She edited the Crusade column in the *Labour Leader* after June 1917 and it is from this paper that the Crusade in Bolton can be tracked. In December 1917, Bolton Women's Peace Crusade held its first meeting, addressed by Lillian Anderson Fenn, the organiser of Liverpool's Women's Peace Crusade. She had spoken at a peace meeting in Bolton's Victoria Square in August 1916, showing local support for the anti-war movement.

Regular Women's Peace Crusade meetings in Bolton continued throughout 1918, with the *Labour Leader* reporting in January, that the branch had sold a number of peace badges and that local membership was increasing. Well-known campaigners such as Edith Snowdon addressed the branch. The *Bolton Journal* of 19 April 1918 reported '*an eloquent address to a large audience*' by the pacifist and Women's Peace Crusader Charlotte Despard who declared that women as mothers '*felt the bitterness of the dreadful slaughter in France [so]that they were now entering on the Peace Crusade*'.

The Peace meetings were often held in the Spinners' Hall *[right]* and would have included women from the Women's Co-operative Guild and the Independent Labour Party. The Independent Labour Party was active in the town but there was also a radical fully independent Bolton Socialist Club which never affiliated to

any national organization. The club had strong educational, social and sporting groups, notably the Clarion Cycling Club. Local socialist and suffrage women were active in the club, notably Cissie Foley, the sister of Alice Foley. The surviving minutes show that Bolton Socialist Club split completely over whether or not to support the First World War. As a result the organisation took no active role on the issue, although the club president John Paulden was a conscientious objector and also a member of the British Socialist Party.

Women's Peace Crusade activist and socialist Annot Robinson spoke at a meeting of Bolton Independent Labour Party on January 13th, 1918. As a suffragist and socialist, Annot Robinson would have also known members of the Bolton Women's Suffrage Society and the Women's International League. There were four WIL meetings in Bolton in 1918.

Nancy Affleck, 38 years old wife of a Kearsley doctor, presided at Bolton WIL meeting in April 1918, when Margaret Ashton congratulated them for *'having a strong and active Bolton branch'*. The wartime minutes of Bolton Suffrage Society record that when the national movement split over issues of war and peace in the spring of 1915, the local Executive voted 9 to 3 to support the proposition that *'the political propaganda of the National Union should be directed for Women's Suffrage only'* [i.e. not for discussing war or peace!] However determined to be neutral on the war issue, they refused to display a recruiting poster at their shop. Locally, suffragist Miss Johnson spoke in support of the national executive members, including Mancunian councillor Margaret Ashton, who had resigned in opposition to the stance on the war. It is clear that the Bolton branch thought highly of Margaret Ashton and in November 1915 the Executive agreed to send her a memorial. Bolton also had a branch of the pacifist United Suffragists, formed in 1916.

There was a lively group of women in Bolton with their roots in suffrage, co-operation and peace. There was a local branch of the Women's International League in the town and the secretaries in 1916 and 1917 were respectively, Miss McNeill and Miss Holden both of Harwood. The president of the Women's Co-operative Guild in Bolton, trade union agitator, poor law Guardian and suffragist, Sarah Reddish, had been one of the 180 women elected to go to The Hague Congress in 1915 and she continued to campaign for peace throughout the war. Her suffragist colleague, socialist and

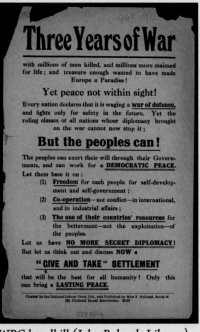

WPC handbill (John Rylands Library)

teacher, Alice Collinge, chaired the meeting of Bolton Women's Peace Crusade in January 1918, when Ethel Snowden addressed a crowded audience at Lower Spinners Hall. Alice Collinge's work brought her into contact with gay rights activist Edward Carpenter, Irish campaigner Countess Markievicz and her sister, the poet Eva Gore Booth. Miss Collinge said she was glad Bolton was 'at last allowing a lady of such intellectual attainments and magnificent courage as Mrs Snowden to enter the town.' (*Bolton Journal* 18 Jan 1918) This suggests that previously Ethel Snowden had been banned or deterred from coming to Bolton and is a rare piece of evidence as to the level of opposition to WPC in Bolton and the barriers set up against it. Other activists were working class socialists Cissy and Alice Foley who were both involved in pacifism and trade union agitation. Their two brothers joined up and the older brother John was killed on the Somme. Alice was also a friend and supporter of local conscientious objector, George Grundy, who was sent to Wormwood Scrubs Prison in 1917. Another socialist activist, Helen Wright (nee Mearns), campaigned against conscription. Her fiancé, William Ewart Wright, was imprisoned as a CO, and they married once he was released in 1919. Helen became the first woman mayor of Bolton.

Suffragist and activist Florence Blincoe came to Bolton in 1913. She was a trade union campaigner, and a Poor Law Guardian who worked with soldiers' wives during the war, arguing against state surveillance and concerned about their well-being. She committed suicide in 1932 after a bout of depression.

Another Radical woman from Bolton: Alice Thomasson

Since the start of the First World War, young cotton mill worker Alice Thomasson had watched the young men she knew join the Colours and go off to fight. She wanted to 'do her bit', but as the eldest of four, her wage as a cop packer was needed at home. Finally, in late 1917, Alice aged 21, decided to join the Women's Army Auxiliary Corps. In May 1918, she was posted to a hospital and army supply depot at Abbeville on the road from Paris to Boulogne, where she was to serve as a general domestic worker. Just three days later tragedy struck. During the night of May 29th-30th, the Germans launched a bombing raid and 8 women, including Alice, were killed outright, whilst another died later of her wounds. [See GM14 blog November 20th 2016] She was buried in France.

Arrests in Rochdale! The 'Jim' Simmons case: *by Pete Gascoigne*

In late September 1917 there was a considerable amount of pro-peace activity taking place in Rochdale. A number of incidents in the town led to at least one meeting of the Women's Peace Crusade in 1917 although the local and hostile *Rochdale Times* argued that: *'To talk of peace by negotiation is as futile as it is dangerous, and we are of opinion that the activities of pacifists in Rochdale have earned for the town a very unenviable reputation'.*

Birmingham Independent Labour Party Federation.

CONSCRIPTION ?

WORKERS !!! Come and insist on the Repeal of the Military Services Acts.

A SERIES OF PUBLIC MEETINGS

Under the auspices of the I.L.P. will be held as under. The Speakers include
R. C. Wallhead (Labour Candidate for Coventry)
C. R. Buxton (Labour Candidate for Accrington)
Corporal Lees-Smith (Ex-M.P. Northampton)
Councillor T. Hackett (Co-op. Candidate Kings Norton)
Ex-Private Jim Simmons (Federation Organiser)

Small Heath. DEFINITE SPEAKERS.
SUNDAY, April 6th, Yardley Road Schools, 6-30 Cpl. LEES-SMITH
FRIDAY ,, 11th, Co-op. Hall, Coventry Rd., 7-30 R. C. WALLHEAD

Kings Heath.
MONDAY, April 7th, Council Schools, High St., 7-30 Cpl. LEES-SMITH

Sparkbrook.
TUESDAY, April 8, Friends' Institute, Moseley Rd., 7-30 Cpl. LEES-SMITH

Rotton Park.
WEDNESDAY, April 9th, Barford Road Schools, 7-30 C'llr. T. HACKETT

Kings Norton.
THURSDAY, Apl. 10th, Stirchley Council Schools, 7-30 R. C. WALLHEAD
SUNDAY ,, 13th, Stirchley Institute, 6-30 - C. R. BUXTON

MOTHERS specially invited. Collection to defray Heavy Expenses.

JOIN the I.L.P. and help to FIGHT CONSCRIPTION

On Saturday 22nd September 1917, there was an advertisement in the more sympathetic *Rochdale Observer* placed by the Friends' (Quakers) Peace Message Committee:

A PUBLIC MEETING will be held in the FRIENDS' MEETING HOUSE George Street, Rochdale,
THIS DAY (Saturday) Sept. 22nd. Chair to be taken by Rev W.D. Lister at 7pm. Mrs HIGGS (of Oldham) and Mr F. GREENWOOD will speak on "A Christian way of Peace and an International Christian Conference." Collections towards expenses.

The same edition also carried an advertisement from the local Independent Labour Party.

Private SIMMONS, on the SQUARE, from Monday to Saturday next, at 6.15pm.
Having been wounded three times and having lost his foot he wants you

*to know what war is. Who frightened the English War Code? Ask Private
Simmons. He is on the Square from MONDAY to SATURDAY at 6.15.*

Who was Private Simmons? Jim Simmons was a Primitive Methodist
local preacher, a professional soldier who joined the army in 1911,
but was wounded soon after the war broke out and sent back home
to Britain in order to convalesce. During his rehabilitation, in Fernhill
Auxiliary Military Hospital in Stacksteads, Lancashire, near some of
the industrial towns of East Lancashire, he preached in local chapels,
speaking against the war and in favour of a negotiated peace. Simmons
re-joined his unit to serve in Gallipoli and Egypt. In Suez, as the
organizer of rank-and-file discussion groups, as the author of an anti-
conscription letter to a Birmingham alderman and the suspected
ringleader of a collective refusal to obey an order, his officers considered
him a threat to army discipline and he was transferred to the western
front. In May 1916 he was shot in the foot at Vimy Ridge; by December
of that year, complications with the wound required the amputation
of the lower third of his leg. Back home, still in uniform, he became
prominent in ILP agitation for a negotiated peace.

On Wednesday 26th September 1917, the *Rochdale Observer* reported:
***ILP Soldier's Defiance: Rochdale Speech Last Night: After Police
Warning*** *'At an Independent Labour Party meeting, attended by several
hundreds of people and held on Rochdale Town Hall Square last night, it
was stated that the police had prohibited Private C J Simmons (Worcester
Regiment), who belongs to Birmingham, from addressing the gathering.
Private Simmons, however, defied the ultimatum and spoke for the best part
of an hour in support of an immediate peace by negotiation. Police officers
who had been present did not interfere with him, and up to a late hour last
night he had not been arrested.'*

However, on Saturday 29th September the *Rochdale Times* reported
that Simmons had been arrested but it then accused the ILP of [being]

'engaged in an unpatriotic campaign, calculated to benefit only the German Emperor and his fellow murderers [and] we suppose that the exploits of the noisy little band of peace-at-any-pricers in this country are made the most of in Germany, and that their speeches are reproduced in the German Press in order to bolster up the drooping morale of the Huns at home'.

On the other hand on Saturday 29th September the *Rochdale Observer* carried advertisements from the Independent Labour Party. '*HELP THE PROTEST in favour of Free Speech on the SQUARE, TO-NIGHT, at 7pm, and get Private Simmons out of prison. **I.L.P., ROCHDALE BRANCH – KEIR HARDY MEMORIAL THE ARREST OF PRIVATE SIMMONS - A GREAT DEMONSTRATION** will be held in the Pioneers' Hall, Toad Lane, **Keep free speech**'*.

Continuing his anti-war campaign as 'Ex-Private Simmons', after being discharged from the army in November 1918, Jim Simmons enlightened his audiences regarding the cruelties of the army's Field Punishment No. 1, commonly referred to as 'crucifixion' because the victim was fixed in a similar position. On the 3rd October the following appeared in the *Rochdale Observer*:
'ARREST OF PRIVATE SIMMONS – PROTEST MEETINGS
On Saturday and Sunday, under the auspices of the Rochdale branch of the Independent Labour Party, protest meetings were held in relation to the arrest of Private Simmons by the military police as a result of strongly-worded speeches on the Town Hall Square last week.'

This was the catalyst for a brief demonstration of the Women's Peace Crusade on Saturday 29th September 1917, led by women from Manchester but which would have been supported by women from the Women's International League (local secretary Mrs Walmsley) and local women from the ILP. Well known women from Manchester were there too, to support the local Crusade.

There was an active branch of the Women's International League in Rochdale which will have organised meetings of the Women's Peace Crusade: its secretary Mrs Walmsley lived in Spotland [now the home of activist Pete Gascoigne and his late partner Paula Kaniuk]. The arrest of Jim Simmons was the catalyst for the local Crusade but there but there were many other local Crusades during the summer 1917 which may have inspired and mobilised Rochdale women.

WOMEN'S PEACE CRUSADE.

A GREAT PEACE DEMONSTRATION
will be held on the
TOWN   HALL   SQUARE,   ROCHDALE,
On Sunday, Sept. 30, at 2-30 p.m.
Chair : Miss E. C. WILKINSON, M.A.
Speaker, Mrs. WATTS, and others.
If wet, the meeting will be held in the Pioneers' Hall,
Toad Lane. Tea will be provided in the I.L.P.
Rooms, Hunter's Lane.   27—9

The *Labour Leader* announced
'A MEETING will be held on the TOWN HALL SQUARE TOMORROW (Sunday 30th September) at 2.30pm.Chair Miss E C WILKINSON M.A. Speakers: Mrs WATTS and Mrs MUTER WILSON. If wet, the Meeting will be held in the Pioneers' Hall: Tea will be provided in the I.L.P. Rooms.' The local press reported:
'WOMEN'S PEACE MEETING ATTEMPT TO BREAK IT UP FAILS.
There were lively scenes on the Rochdale Town Hall Square, on Sunday afternoon, when an attempt was made to break up a meeting arranged in connection with the Women's Peace Crusade. Several men were parted by the police. The meeting was presided over by Miss E.C. Wilkinson, M.A. of

Manchester, and addresses on peace were delivered by Mrs Watts and Mrs Muter Wilson (also of Manchester).Mrs Watts pleaded for all to unite in the cry for a peace without indemnities or annexation, and one founded on the spirit of brotherhood. During Mrs Muter Wilson's address there was an interruption amongst the crowd and Miss Wilkinson, addressing the audience, said there were present a certain section of men who had been ordered to break up the meeting. If the meeting kept solid this could not be done.'

The noise at one end of the crowd, however, gradually grew louder. It was stated to be caused by some men from outside the town. One Rochdale man, an old soldier, who declared that his age was 67 years, and that he had several sons in the Army, was a frequent interrupter. The disturbers concentrated their attention on a group of Independent Labour Party men, and roundly accused them, in strong language, of being shirkers, conscientious objectors and traitors. Wild threats were used and it was difficult to hear what Mrs Wilson said. Numerous attempts were made to surround the interrupters and rush them away.

At the close of the meeting Miss Wilkinson put a resolution protesting the arrest of Private Simmons, who spoke on the Square on Tuesday night.

Drawing by Emily Johns 2016

Splendid Bradford! *by Eve Haskins*

*'During WW1, Bradford was a hive of radicalism and the [Humanity]
League were very much part of the emancipation movement. Women
over the age of 30 did not get the vote until years later - which in itself
gives significance to the 3,000 women who attended this [Women's Peace
Crusade] It was ahead of its time.'* Bradford Peace Museum: 2016.

In June 1917, the *Labour Leader* started a regular column about the
newly revitalised Women's Peace Crusade. In September 1917, referring
to the first mass demonstration of the Bradford women under the
banner of the Women's Peace Crusade, the column reported that:
*"The Bradford women are splendid. They attribute their success on Sunday
to their open air meetings at street corners. They have held three of these
every week since June."*

The demonstration marched with
banners from the Textile Hall in
Westgate to Carlton Street for a rally
in the Textile School grounds. The
Bradford Pioneer hailed the Crusade
as a 'huge success'. In Bradford there
was a group established by Mrs.
Barbour of Woodlands Road called
the 'Mothers and Wives of Bradford
Conscientious Objectors', revealing

*Banner making c 1915 (Working Class
Movement Library)*

widespread anti-war feeling in the area. By October 1917, the well-
known Quaker pacifist and socialist Isabella Ford, reported that the
Bradford women helped the Women's Peace Crusade in Leeds also: *"…
representatives from Bradford… have worked with us and helped us most
splendidly"*.

Neighbouring Shipley was another centre of radicalism in 1917, with branches of the Bradford Women's Humanity League, of The Women's International League and the No-Conscription Fellowship. There was also a Shipley Council against Conscription. Bradford activists, socialists and suffragists Fanny Muir and Esther Sandiforth were members of the council as well as being members of the Shipley branch of the influential ILP.

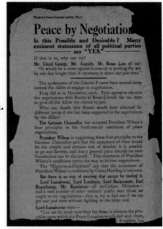

WPC Handbill 1917 (John Rylands Library)

Muir was arrested under the Defence of the Realm regulations in May 1918 for speaking in public against the war and although the weekly meetings of the Women's Peace Crusade continued, it was not until Muir's release from prison in August 1918 that the *Bradford Pioneer* carried an advertisement for another 'Mass Demonstration' of the WPC. The paper also reported on 27th September 1918 a 'Welcome Home Social' for Muir, planned by the Bradford Women's Humanity League. It also reported that the same week Muir had spoken at a public meeting in Bradford, following a large demonstration throughout the city.

Although there are reports of Muir working with the local branch of the ILP in October 1918, after this time she disappears from public record.

But the story didn't end there: in January 1918 at least two Crusades were organised – one took place despite the Yorkshire weather! *"A very successful open-air meeting was held on Sunday, despite the cold, damp weather, by the Bradford Women's Peace Crusade. The keen enthusiasm of the audience was an inspiration to all responsible for the effort"* while the next week *"Miss Wilson Wilson of 'The New Crusader' addressed a crowded meeting of the Bradford Women's Peace Crusade on the Women's*

Army Auxiliary Corps". This was Theodora Wilson Wilson, from Cumbria, a well-known Quaker author and campaigner for peace. The *New Crusader* had been started in 1916 by Wilfred Wellock a CO from Nelson and, when he was imprisoned, Mrs Wilson Wilson took over the editorship.

In March 1918 Lillian Anderson Fenn, the wife of a Liverpool CO and another well-known Crusade speaker, visited Bradford, where she held her audience spell-bound for an hour, and the resolution regarding the need to eradicate militarism from schools, was unanimously adopted. *'Bradford is to hold a mass meeting on March 17, when Mrs Despard will be the principal speaker'*

And this was a great success – the *Labour Leader* reported that:
"The news of the Bradford women's great peace demonstration on 17th March arrived too late for last week's issue. Readers will rejoice to learn that a fine procession, headed by a band and peace banners marched through the principal streets of the town and met with many signs of earnest sympathy. Although there was no tram service scores of women walked miles to take part in it. The Temperance Hall meeting, which followed, was addressed by Mrs Despard and was crowded and enthusiastic."

Bradford women meant to continue their propaganda till the people realise their responsibility for the continuance of the war and they were instrumental in developing the Crusade across Yorkshire so that by July 1918, the *Labour Leader* reported that *"A Women's Peace Crusade has started in Halifax, with Miss D. Yates, 11 Heath Avenue, as Secretary. The Colne Crusade reports two well attended and highly successful open air meetings, held during the last two weeks, one addressed by Miss Wilson, of Bradford, and the other by Miss McKay of Ilkley"*.

Women were supporting each other by travelling across the country to speak out publicly about the need for a just and negotiated peace.

Imprisoned! Fanny Muir: Widow with children! And her activist friend – Esther Sandiford.

These two women Fanny Muir of Frizinghall, Bradford and Esther Sandiforth of Windhill, Shipley, were both middle aged women with children. Fanny was widowed by the time they set up the Bradford Women's Humanity League in 1916, in opposition to the passing of the first Military Service Bill. The BWHL was one of the first groups in the country to become involved with the Women's Peace Crusade in 1917, and Muir was influential in setting up the Shipley branch of the WPC in 1917. Shipley seems to have been a centre of radicalism in 1917, and as well as the BWHL there were women

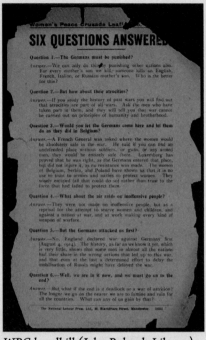

WPC handbill (John Rylands Library)

living there who were also members of the Women's International League and the No-Conscription Fellowship. There was also a Shipley Council against Conscription, and both Muir and Sandiforth were supporters of this, as well as being members of the Shipley branch of the influential ILP. The *Labour Leader* claims that the first Bradford Crusade attracted 3000 women and some men, and stated: *'The motives of Muir and Sandiforth in their anti-war work mirrored those of many mainly working class women in the country at the time: they were angry at the slaughter of their men in the trenches and elsewhere, this anger being fuelled by forced conscription and the rising casualty lists, as well as the high food prices, food shortages and enduring queues on the home front.'*

Fanny Muir was a pacifist and campaigned for a negotiated peace throughout the war. In May 1918 the *Bradford Daily Telegraph* reported that she was arrested after addressing a meeting of 100 people at the Market Place in Shipley. She was charged under the Defence of the Realm Act and imprisoned for 3 months for public order offences.

Esther Sandiforth was a regular speaker at the Crusade in Bradford but was not arrested. She was also the organiser of the Crusade in Bradford and included in the *Labour Leader's* 1917 WPC directory of organisers.

Drawing by Emily Johns 2016

Cumberland and Westmorland: New and active Peace Crusades! *by Hilary Chuter*

Blackpool c1914

By the summer of 1917 Women's Peace Crusade groups were appearing across the North West of England. In August there was reference to activity in Blackpool (*Labour Leader*, 9 August 1917). In September the Directory of the WPC listed a contact for Kendal, and another for Carlisle (*Labour Leader*, 27 September 1917). In May 1918 it was reported that '*new and active Peace Crusades have been started at Barrow-in-Furness, Norwich, Exeter, Rothwell and Market Harborough*' (*Labour Leader*, 8 November 1917 and 30 May 1918). In October 1918 there was a Women's Peace Crusade meeting in Ulverston, which '*was molested by a band of men*' (*Labour Leader*, 10 October 1918).

The *Labour Leader*, in its Women's Peace Crusade column, reported a series of meetings held in Blackpool in August 1917:

'On Blackpool sands, Mrs Louis [Lillian] Anderson Fenn, who is devoted to our work, speaking on Sunday for the Civil Liberties Society, and on Monday evening for the I.L.P [Independent Labour Party], held a huge crowd for over two hours, and a Blackpool comrade, calling in at our office, described it as one of the most wonderful meetings of his life. "The people are eager for the message women like Mrs Fenn bring them," he said. "The crowd was made up of well-paid workers and soldiers, yet she carried them all with her. The Women's Peace Crusade is just what is wanted." He carried off a big parcel of our leaflets for distribution.'

The Labour Leader printed a directory of local Crusade organisers in the summer of 1917 and the Carlisle organiser was Mrs. Martha McNaughton, 12 Crummock Street, Carlisle, married to Daniel McNaughton. Daniel was a tin biscuit box maker who probably worked for Hudson Scott and Sons, James Street, Carlisle. Although no profession is given for Martha, it is likely that she was a suffrage woman with some connections to the ILP. In 1917 she was in her early 40s and had 3 young children at home. Daniel's job may well have been a reserved occupation. The other organiser in the Lake District was Mrs Braithwaite of Ghyll Close, Kendal, a large house built in 1868 for a local Quaker woollen merchant, Charles Lloyd Braithwaite, and his wife, Susanna Wilson. In 1911 Isaac Braithwaite, Charles's son, inherited the property, and 'Mrs Braithwaite' is Isaac's wife, Mary Snowden Braithwaite.

Mary Snowden Braithwaite, née Thomas, was born into a Quaker family in Baltimore in 1851. Although Isaac and Mary married in Baltimore in1890: by the outbreak of war they lived in Kendal and were active Quakers.

Mary Snowden Braithwaite: [courtesy Woodbrooke archive]

Mary and Isaac were in Kendal in 1914. There is mention of Mary in a list of subscribers to the Women's International League for the year ending August 1918 and this would have been her link to the Crusade locally.

Her family connections also make it likely. Her sister-in-law, Anna Braithwaite Thomas, was in England during the First World War '*where she served on the Alien's Committee and a relief mission to Vienna, Austria, after the War.*' Her niece, Dr Henrietta Martha Thomas, was involved in pacifist service in Germany and Austria and writing accounts of her work in the *Labour Leader* before she died in 1919. Although there is no specific evidence of Women's Peace Crusade activity in Kendal, other than the mention of Mrs Braithwaite, it does show that women were part of a much wider network of pacifist and anti-militarist women in Cumberland and Westmorland during the war.

There were No-Conscription Fellowship branches in Shap and Penrith. Mabel Phythian kept a journal of a tour to the Lake District that she had made in the summer of 1916 with her undergraduate friends Nic and Regina Brogan. They had to register at the police station in Penrith under DORA regulations but they had been invited to a meeting of the local branch of the NCF where she noted that '*the group keen but as usual suspected and hampered and some more courageous in their counsel than others.*' while Catherine Marshall's mother, after attending a meeting of the Penrith NCF in September 1916 stated, '*the NCF man is a tailor, he was elected onto the local [military] tribunal but they would not have him*'. While across the country there were a series of safe houses being set up for COs to take refuge, although people were anxious about their own involvement in this process. Catherine Marshall's mother in Keswick, asked '*Can you guarantee due notice of arrest?*' while Margaret Irwin in Cockermouth asked, '*By taking him in I suppose I expose myself to the possibility of arrest for harbouring a deserter, though of course there would be no attempt to conceal him.*' The draconian Defence of the Realm Act even reached the Lake District.

Munitions worker c 1917

The Women's Peace Crusade had been formed in Barrow in the spring of 1918. In June 'two open air meetings were held which proved strikingly successful. Mrs Helen Crawfurd addressed huge and attentive crowds on the square and created such a deep impression that little opposition was shown. Numbers of special constables and detectives were present, whose services, however, were not required. The collections were good and new members were enrolled' (Labour Leader, 27 June 1918). The Labour Leader advertised in autumn 1918 that 'Miss Hague will be in Barrow from September 28 till October 6. If any town near Barrow would like to have a Women's Peace Crusade I should be glad to consider the possibility of helping to start one' (Labour Leader, 19 September 1918). Nora Hague was a seasoned anti-war campaigner, active in the Derby branch of the WPC. Circumstances had allowed her to take on the role of travelling organiser. In 1917 she was sacked from her job as a teacher because 'The committee [Derbyshire Education Committee] endorsed the action of the governors of Ilkeston Secondary School in dismissing Miss Nora Hague, assistant mistress, for distributing *pacifist literature.'* It was stated that there was nothing against her professionally and that what she did was from a high sense of religious duty.

The Independent Labour Party and Ilkeston Trades Council wrote to the Committee *'protesting against the governor's action'* (*Derbyshire Courier*, 22 December 1917). But by March 1918 she was organising for the Peace Crusade-*'excellent reports are reaching us of Miss Hague's work in the Midlands'* and she was soon the Midlands organiser. (*Labour Leader*, 14 March and 21 March 1918). By May 1918 she is described as 'the National Organiser' (*Labour Leader* 16 May 1918).

In August, before she started her organising in the Barrow area, as a result of her *'indefatigable work ... several new crusades have been started in the villages around Leicester'* (*Labour Leader* 29 August 1918).

By October 1918 *'Miss Nora Hague reports on her progress in the Barrow area, where she has had village meetings and has addressed gatherings of the Cooperative Guilds, Women's Labour Leagues and the National Federation of Women Workers. At Ulverston the meeting was "molested by a band of men who prevented our getting any kind of hearing – the police ordered us out of the room we had hired, while our audience sat perfectly quiet waiting to hear us but unable to do so because of the organised band." Miss Hague finds the women of the crusade keen and enthusiastic.'* (*Labour Leader*, 10 October 1918).

It would seem that Nora Hague single-handedly helped to organise many of the crusades up and down the country.

Blackburn: 'A People's Peace – a Peace that would abide' by Dr. Alison Ronan.

Research by Hayley Wells (photos from Blackburn Library)

'The women of Blackburn have for some time back taken up the question of Peace vigorously.....and they are striving to make Peace the ruling thought with the population of Blackburn.' (*Labour Leader* August 1917)

In 1916, there had been an outcry in Darwen, the neighbouring town to Blackburn, about the ill-treatment and torture of a number of Darwen COs. The case was taken up by the town's Labour MP, Philip Snowden. Many men from nearby Accrington in the local Pals Regiment had died at the Somme as had local men from Blackburn and Darwen so the local towns had various reasons to welcome the Women's Peace Crusade in 1917. But it wasn't all plain sailing.

The first meeting on August 6th had attracted a crowd of over 1500 although there was a '*great deal of disturbance*'. Local weaver Miss Houlker presided (probably Caroline or May Houlker from Accrington whose brother Albert was in the Accrington Pals regiment) and Crusade activist, Manchester councillor and Women's International League organiser, Margaret Ashton was present. She spoke of the importance of internationalism and the underlying socialism of the Women's Peace Crusade, '*The Women of the world had nothing against each other… .in the belligerent countries women were gathering and trying to make common cause against the horror and slaughter decimating the nations that were at war. [Women] had been kept out of the government of the world which was controlled by men, in the interest chiefly, of capitalists and property owners.*' (*Blackburn Times* August 11th 1917) There was constant heckling but the Crusaders were undeterred.

In early September 1917 Sylvia Pankhurst attracted a crowd of over 2000 in two meetings on the Market Place although there was '*considerable booing.*' She talked about the internationalism of the movement as well and the need for the rights of democracy in all countries. Local women chaired these meetings, both Mary Hopwood of Holly Street (wife of a cotton operative and mother of a conscientious objector, Edwin Hopwood) and Eliza Brindle, a weaver of Lower Darwen whose son John had been killed at the Somme, presided at most of the meetings although the local organiser

Portrait of Margaret Ashton

of the Crusade was 'fancy' weaver Miss Lydia Leach. There was clearly a small group of committed women, mostly weavers, who gave up their time for the Crusade. Mrs. Brindle declared that '*the flower of the nation was being butchered for goodness knows what: not for democracy, she thought.*' (*Blackburn Times* September 15th 1917) but there were constant interruptions, particularly from women whose men were at the Front.

The Crusade women were trying hard to involve other women's organisations and local clergy but as the *Labour Leader* reported '*these efforts have had a somewhat mixed reception.*' The HQ for the Crusade was the ILP institute on Freckleton Street, Blackburn showing the strong links between the Crusade and the socialist anti-militarist movement in the town. There was a sizable number of conscientious objectors in Blackburn and Darwen, many of them from the ILP but reaction to them was mixed, as a letter from weaver Walter Duckworth to the Blackburn Times in October 1917, shows: '*... COs are not looked upon as martyrs with halos but rather as traitors.*'

Women were travelling across the county to support the Crusade, Mrs. Aldersley, another weaver from Nelson, spoke about the power of women coming together and declared that she was '*prepared to march to London and appeal to parliament that the war should be stopped.*' (*Blackburn Times* October 13th 1917) The Blackburn Crusade continued into 1918. Charlotte Despard spoke in January 1918 arguing strongly against the idea of a '*knockout blow or a crushing of Germany.*' In February, Quaker Mrs. Watts of Manchester, spoke to the Crusade, in a meeting presided over by local Quaker, Kathleen Davies, who was friend of Lydia Leach's. The meeting focused on the Representation of the People Act and some women being able to vote in the next general Election, '*[Women] were determined that it should be the beginning of a new era ... it was up to them to see that such a war as this should never happen again.*' (*Blackburn Times* February 2nd 1918)

Increasingly the Crusade found it hard to find places to hold their meetings: Accrington Town Hall was refused and in Blackburn the council, several churches, chapels and Temperance societies had refused their rooms as well. The Market Place and the ILP rooms continued to be regular meeting sites. Late in October 1917, Eva Gore Booth and her companion Esther Roper came to Blackburn calling on the government *'to cease the tremendous wastage of human life.'* These two women, seasoned suffrage and trade union activists, were well known as supporters of the Crusade and for supporting men at the Military Tribunals, who were claiming exemption from military service on the grounds of conscience. Another well-known speaker in Blackburn in February 1918, was Isabella Ford, the Crusade organiser for Leeds, a renowned suffragist, Women's International League activist and pacifist. As the war drew to its close, Blackburn Council refused the Town Hall for the ILP annual social. It was never easy to be anti-war.

Town Hall, Blackburn c 1914

The local Blackburn Women's Peace Crusade organiser was the young socialist and trade union activist Lydia Leach – working locally in the mills as a 'fancy' weaver. She played a leading part in co-ordinating the Crusades across Blackburn. She was self-educated and committed to feminist and socialist causes. Her sweetheart, Ernest Flint, was in prison as a conscientious objector so Lydia would have been involved in local campaigns against conscription. She was also a member of the local radical Women's Adult School, taking night school courses

in history and economics. Because she felt so passionately about peace and anti-militarism, she gave up a course of teacher training in Birmingham, and returned to the mill, working to support the Crusade and agitate for the release of COs.

Incensed by wartime food prices, and profiteering, she represented Blackburn Trades and Labour Council on the local Food Control Committee and Profiteering Committee. She was a member of the After Care Committee concerned with the wartime employment of children and, as secretary of the Blackburn Women's Council, she took a leading part in the movement for the institution of children's play centres. When Ernest was released in 1919 they got married and moved to Spring Vale garden village in Darwen, a settlement managed by the co-operator, Corder Catchpool, another CO, and committed pacifist and anti-fascist. Lydia was the first woman to stand for election (unsuccessfully) as a socialist on Blackburn Town Council and she was consistently active in local politics and trade union activism.

Ghandi in Darwen 1931

Engineer Ernest was also a trade union activist and it is very likely that both he and Lydia would have met Gandhi in 1931, when he was invited to Darwen by Catchpool. As part of the Quit India campaign to end British rule in the sub-continent, Gandhi had urged Indians to boycott cotton goods which, in turn, had devastating effects on Lancashire cotton workers with thousands losing their jobs. Although Catchpool's invitation was intended to show Gandhi the error of the boycott, he was received warmly by the local Darwen workers, who, instead, blamed the greed of mill owners for their plight. Lydia continued to campaign for peace throughout her life. She died in 1934.

Much of this information has come from (Northern Daily Telegraph Obituary 1934)

Internationalist Burnley and 'Red' Nelson: August and September 1917: *by Dr. Alison Ronan.*
Research by Sue Nike and Denise North

*Nelson Independent Labour Party
conscientious objectors 1916*

*Lift up the people's banner
And let the ancient cry
For justice and for freedom
Re-echo to the sky.'*
[Song sung at Burnley WPC August 1917]

By 1917, images of grief and roll calls of casualty figures were a regular item in the socialist paper the *Labour Leader*. In the weaving towns of Burnley and Nelson, local papers were full of pictures of the dead.

In August the women of Nelson, led by local socialists Selina Cooper and Gertrude Ingham mobilised over 1500 women, planning their Peace Crusade meeting in a crowded Co-op Hall on Albert Street. The chair of the meeting was Deborah Smith, wife of a weaver, who talked of her sons on the Front, one wounded, and another, Rennie, who was an ex-student of the radical Ruskin College and now a prisoner of war. The Crusade was essentially internationalist and, for Deborah Smith, this may have been encouraged by her son, Rennie's pre-war work on the staff of the International Trade Union Secretariat which had its offices in Berlin.

Women with sons and husbands at the front campaigned alongside the families of conscientious objectors. Nelson and Burnley had one of the largest numbers of COs in the country.

On Saturday August 11th 1917, a huge crowd of more than 2000 women and girls marched through Nelson up Bradley Road and Manchester Road to the recreation ground, carrying banners representing the Labour Church and Socialist Sunday School. Women from the local branch of Sylvia Pankhurst's Workers Suffrage Society carried a banner 'We want peace and no rest till we get it.' Other banners read 'We demand a People's Peace' and 'Hail the Russian Revolution!'

A crowd of over 20,000 people had gathered to hear Lancashire 'mill girl poetess' and socialist Ethel Carnie Holdsworth, Lillian Anderson Fenn and trade union and suffrage activist Margaret Bondfield from London. The crowd cheered and booed and there was a great deal of opposition – hostile elements singing 'God save the King' and 'Keep the Home Fires Burning' but Miss Lucy Ingham, one of the organisers declared, 'I feel so proud of our women: they were so brave and walked unflinchingly along – are we downhearted? Not we!' Her brother Alex was a conscientious objector in Wormwood Scrubs and her mother, Gertrude Ingham, a founder member of the town's Independent Labour Party alongside the better known Selina Cooper. In late August there were two large Crusade meetings held on the Market ground in Burnley and then in the Co-op Hall, where more than 500 women came to the meeting, sung The Red Flag and collected over £5. Over 100 women signed up to become members of the local branch of the Crusade,

In September 1917, Ethel Snowden came to Nelson; Selina Cooper chaired the meeting and over 1200 women crowded into Salem Street School. Selina Cooper was a driving force in Nelson and like many anti-war campaigners she worked on several committees organising relief work. Although willing to help people suffering from the consequences of the war, Selina, who was a pacifist, refused to take part in army recruiting campaigns. She was totally opposed to military conscription and, after its introduction in 1916, became involved in helping those men who were sent to prison for refusing to fight. She worked closely with Gertrude Ingham. They had both been founding members of the Socialist hall on Vernon Street and both were active in the No-Conscription Fellowship. Nelson was a hotbed of anti-conscription feeling and many ILP men refused to fight. In the village of Roughlee, just outside Nelson stands the Clarion House, one of several 'Clarion Houses' that were used by the Nelson Independent Labour Party. Men on the run from the military during WW1 might use the clubhouse to lie low for a few days.

The Crusade continued throughout the autumn 1917: another 102 women enrolled at a Burnley meeting where Isabella Ford spoke on November 18 and, as the leaflets had been banned under the new DORA regulations, the women suggested buying the radical papers, the *Leader* the *Daily Herald* and so on, to distribute. locally.

As Selina Cooper said

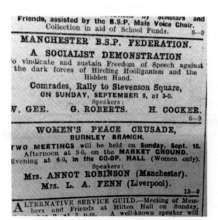

'Those that took part did something wonderful. It is one thing to come to a meeting, another thing to march through the street to be jeered at and booed at. When the settlement comes, every woman who joined the Crusade will be glad to will be glad to say 'I joined the Crusade!'

International socialists from Burnley and Nelson: *Nancy Shimbles, Gertrude Ingham* and *Deborah Smith*

Nancy Shimbles' house
74, Carleton Street Nelson
Drawing by Emily Johns

In July 1917, one of Nelson's socialist and pacifist agitators, local weaver Nancy Shimbles, died aged just 38.

> '*Like Keir Hardie, she loved the workers in every land, the poor and oppressed all, over Europe.*'

Many Independent Labour Party members attended the funeral. The whole network of the anti-war movement came to remember her activism – there were the local members of the ILP, women from the Women's International League and the Women's Co-operative Guild, members of the No-Conscription Fellowship, the ILP Sunday School, the Board of Guardians, the local Weavers and her 'workmates'[sic].

There were wreaths from Miss Cowgill from the WCG, from Mrs. Wellock, whose husband was in prison as a CO and from many others who would have supported Nancy's anti-war stance.

The Women's Peace Crusades in Nelson were held in her memory. There was a huge groundswell of anti-war feeling in the town. There were letters in the local papers, supporting the stand of conscientious objector and Christian pacifist, Wilfred Wellock, from Ethel Carnie and from

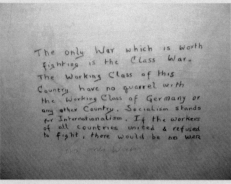

The only War which is worth fighting is the Class War. The Working Class of this Country have no quarrel with the Working Class of Germany or any other Country. Socialism stands for Internationalism. If the workers of all countries united & refused to fight, there would be no WAR

Graffiti from COs in Richmond Castle 1916

Deborah Smith. Deborah Smith worked alongside the local socialist pacifist women although her own sons had gone to war.

Nancy worked alongside another activist, Gertrude Ingham, whose son was imprisoned but who had also worked closely with Selina Cooper to set up the Independent Labour Party in Nelson. Nancy was part of a wider network of socialist women across East Lancashire agitating for a better future.

Front of Socialist Institute, Nelson
Drawing by Emily Johns

The people's flag is deepest red
It shrouded oft our martyred dead
And ere their limbs grew stiff and cold
Their hearts' blood dyed to every fold
…
Though cowards flinch and traitors sneer
We'll keep the red flag flying here

Making the script for 'CRUSADING WOMEN'
by *Hazel Roy*

Going back 100 years is challenging. Many of the pioneer women who courageously opposed WW1 have disappeared from history and while every young history student has heard of Mrs. Pankhurst, there is far less material available to tell the story of the women who opposed her stance on the war. Thanks to the tenacity of Alison Ronan and our other researchers, piecing together the jigsaw was tremendously satisfying even if at times we had to make calculated guesses about who would have been at certain rallies, and who would have known each other. There is plenty to support the conjecture that thrown together in adversity, the bonds of friendship were strong throughout the movement and what has been fascinating is to see the link between the anti-war campaign and the early socialist movement. These women were not just campaigning for peace, they wanted a better world for the poor and underprivileged, votes for women but also the right to join trade unions and challenge capitalism. Several, like Phillis Skinner, went to prison for treason, divorced or were divorced by their husbands, had relationships with CO's and pioneered many different freedoms for women, both in their dress, in their lifestyle and in their beliefs.

Time and time again, I found myself astounded by their courage, faced with a wall of opposition, and often physically violent crowds fired up with patriotic zeal. While Alison provided dozens of small human details, which helped bring the characters to life and ensure they were more than a mouthpiece for stirring anti-war speeches, wherever possible we used the text of the actual speeches to provide authenticity. I hope I was successful breathing life into the linking dialogue. I was particularly pleased to discover, when I was preparing Helena Swanwick's speech, that Siegfried Sassoon's powerful anti-war Declaration to the Government produced in July 1917 had been published in full in just one newspaper, the *Bradford Pioneer*, before the government banned it, so our millworkers would have been familiar with his view that the war was being unnaturally prolonged by those who had the power to end it.

I wish we could have done more and made a longer film but I hope the book will supplement any missing details and that this collaboration will continue, as there is so much more to discover. I particularly hope that we can make the film widely available to secondary schools and young people generally, as I can think of few more inspirational models than the WWI campaigning pacifists and it is time their story was told.

Crusading Women 2016 Photo courtesy of Charlotte Bill

Making the film *by Charlotte Bill*

I met Alison Ronan part way through making the documentary *These Dangerous Women* which was about the women who tried to stop World War 1 in 1915. We realised there was more to say about the anti-war women in the North West. Alison lent me her book *A Small but Vital Flame* and told me about the Women's Peace Crusade. We decided to work together and applied for a grant from AHRC.

Alison was clear about wanting to make a drama telling the stories of these anti-war women who lived in various weaving towns across the North West and came together to campaign against the war. She recruited volunteer researchers in each town and helped them to start their research. They began unearthing stories from local newspapers, archives and personal letters. We would have meetings where people would share what they had discovered. We began to piece together the story which was turned into a script.

It was important to everyone that we got to as many of the real locations as possible but Oldham Town Hall was under scaffolding: a motorway had been built through Nelson, so we had to adapt our plans.

I began looking at all the archive film which had been made between 1900 and 1920 in the North West. There was much more archive footage than I expected and North West Film Archive were very helpful and generous in finding other pieces. I wanted to have as much documentary in the film as possible. Mill workers leaving the factory gates, Whit processions, Suffragettes addressing the election crowds in Bolton, cotton bales loading at the docks. I decided to shoot the drama in a style which would intercut with the archive footage.

The script had been written in a very theatrical way so it was my job to put some more filmic elements in. Working with director of photography Nick Gordon Smith we looked for a cinematic way to move between the stagey scenes.

We used archive footage which was as close to accurate as possible, locations as accurate as possible and let the acting be as if the ghosts of the past were manifesting in the present. We decided not to exclude cars, satellite dishes and passersby but to let them see the past in their home towns. We attempted to reveal the past in the present and show the ghosts of those who went before us.

We had two wonderful choirs who came and sang in costume, we had friends, families and accidental participants all taking part. It was an incredible experience for everyone, I think, and the rain held off. I hope the film shows the women of the past and present getting together to make the world *a better place.*

Mabel Phythian and Meg Tout (played by Florence King and Eve Francis) Photo courtesy of Charlotte Bill

Working Script

Crusading Women 1917 [edited in the film]

Main Characters

Mabel Pythian	**age 20s** *University student*
Meg Tout	**age 20s** *University student*
Miss Ashton	**age 61** *Manchester City Councillor*
Eve Gore-Booth	**age 47** *Anglo-Irish aristocrat: sister of Countess Markievicz*
Charlotte Despard	**age 71** *Social reformer: Sir John French was her brother*
Lydia Leach	**age 20s** *Weaver socialist pacifist*
Mrs Mary Hopwood	**age 48** *Married to textile worker. Son CO*
Emma Quarmby	**age 20/30s** *Teacher sacked for pacifist views*
Mrs Gertrude Ingham	**age 51** *3 CO son in prison. Husband engineer*
Women in Crowd	**late 40s**
Mrs Helena Swanwick	**age 53** *Committed suicide 1939. Walter Sickert, the painter, was her brother*

MANCHESTER 1917 Peaceful Demo

Mabel Pythian is seen cycling through Alexandra Park *(camera mounted on basket of bike – we just see her hands on the handlebars and we hear her voice singing)*

Mabel: *(sings)* "Sing a song of Europe/highly civilized/ four and twenty nations wholly hypnotized/ if the battle opens/And the bullets start to sing" – *(breaks off to call out to Meg Tout also on a bicycle:)* Meg! They're you are – I'd forgotten we were meeting by the temperance fountain. *(Mabel gets off her bike and wheels it along next to Meg)* I'm so glad you could get away – where have you been hiding?

Meg: Deep in an essay on Napoleon's strategies – it has to be handed in two days from now – *(sees Mabel frown)* Which does not mean to say I am not equally worried about what is happening in this war right now. It's different for you, in a Hall of Residence, but when you live at home and have a leading professor for a father, you're rather obliged to knuckle down. My lovely tutor Miss Sheavyn engineered my escape this morning – she knows how important this demo is for us all. She's marched for the vote often enough and she knows Miss Ashton. But forgive me Mabel – is there any news of your brother Wilfred?

Mabel: *(looking pensive)* Nothing. Look at this Meg *(pulls newspaper from her bike basket)* The *Labour Leader* says that 23,000 have been killed or wounded in the last week alone. Can that be true? Whenever I see the telegram boy I get a sinking feeling – will it be my brother next? It's my worst nightmare. *(Meg reaches out and squeezes her hand; Mabel wipes away a tear roughly)*. That's why we need this Women's Crusade for Peace – to get the women of Manchester out on the streets like they have in Glasgow. Miss Ashton told me how the Glasgow women took on their landlords. They had thousands out last summer, banging dustbin lids on the streets and pouring flour over the landlords to frighten them away. And they've got the council to fix the rents! They're not just suffragists they're socialists too!

Look! I think I can see Miss Ashton up Ahead! (*Waves. Miss Ashton waves back*) Yes it is her! Funny how she used to frighten me once, but she's so kind when you get to know her. She always asks after Wilfred (*rallies*) …they call her the Women's Champion in Bolton you know. She's chairing the speakers today.

Meg: I thought we were to have a band today.

Mabel: We were until the band decided they were not prepared to play for peace – can you believe that? But they'll not deprive us of music. The Clarion singers have rallied - they're even singing a special song about Mary Quaile today. Do you remember her? What a great trade unionist. Do you know how hard she has fought to get the women in munitions a fair wage- even though she's a pacifist herself. She's even got Miss Ashton on a committee. She says she is sickened by the fact that bosses shouting the loudest patriotic slogans are those making the biggest profit out of war, yet they're paying these women a pittance. And many are widows with children - making bombs to make other women widows. It's insane.

Meg: Talking of children I was thinking of Phillis Skinner's little boy. What a shame she isn't here. What a speech she would have made – I have never known anyone so fearless- she's a real diehard Socialist! That would attract some attention, a divorcee marrying a much younger CO! With both her and poor Alan in prison – they say he might lose a leg – who is looking after their little boy Jack?

Mabel: He's being cared for by comrades in the movement – he's only two but such a charmer! You know Maude Hayes is in prison with Phillis – they're both in love with COs. I heard her husband has died but not before she had run away with young Mr Rodway.

Meg: Another scandal in the offing? Oh look! Here comes the choir.

(Choir filmed at the rally singing song to Mary Quaile)

(On the steps facing the crowd Margaret Ashton introduces Eva Gore Booth)

Margaret Ashton: We are lucky to have Miss Gore-Booth here today. She and her companion Miss Roper are no strangers to the women of Manchester (*huge cheer*) They are dedicating themselves to the Crusade and to challenge the Military Tribunals over the conscience clause. Welcome Miss Gore Booth (*enthusiastic applause*)

Eva Gore-Booth: I bring you greetings today sisters and brothers from my sister Constance Markievicz, imprisoned once more for working against the conscription of troops to fight this imperialist war (*heckling "Fenian cowards" easily quelled by the crowd*).

(Fade to end of speech …)

Permanent peace is not possible under the present competitive system but only through co-operation in enterprise. We say to all those campaigning for Peace – end this war of domination – Workers of the world unite for Peace and let us work to create a society of international understanding (*Gives clenched fist salute*)

(*Applause*)

Meg: Is that Charlotte Despard about to speak now?

Mabel: Well I know no-one else who wears a lace mantilla and sandals – she always reminds me of a Goya painting. It is ironic isn't it that she should have founded this campaign when her Brother General French is chief of staff to the British Army.

Meg: Well so many brave women have had to sever the ties of family and marriage taking a stand against this war, just as we've long faced a fight within our families over votes for women.

Miss Ashton: Ladies you will all recognise Mrs Despard who has given her life to campaign for women's rights and peace. She is here today to support the Crusade. Please give her a warm welcome (*applause*)

Charlotte Despard: (*raises a hand to silence them*) Women of Manchester I am here to tell you that I have decided to devote all my time to the Women's Peace Crusade – a democratic crusade which give all women free speech. (*huge applause*) Make no mistake! We women are the only hope to bring peace to this country. It is absolutely essential that women take up the question of peace to try and bring this awful slaughter and misery to an end. As non-combatants they cannot call us cowards – we are out for a peace by negotiation, a people's peace, a lasting peace. (*Fades*)

Mabel: (*whispers to Meg*) She's as fiery as Mrs Swanwick isn't she? Will you excuse me Meg – I'm going over to catch Agnes Whittaker from Longsight ILP who organised today. She seems to have involved a lot of her fellow weavers from the mills. It's quite impressive given she's no older than us. I'm hoping to meet lots of her recruits in the next few days. I am going to follow the crusade to Blackburn and Nelson, to hear Miss Lydia Leach – she's another weaver. She can take your breath away as a speaker and not at all shy! (*Pause*) Miss Shimble's death is a terrible blow though – another great campaigner gone. She was only 38. They reckon the conditions in the Mill sent her to any early grave. No wonder Mary Quaile is fighting for these women. I hope I'll get to Bolton and Rochdale too. They've a lot of support from the Methodists in Bolton – it's good to know some men of God are opposing the war. And the others call themselves Christians!

I will send you postcards Meg…

Meg: I wish I was coming with you – your postcards will be a welcome relief from wretched Napoleon. At least I'll get an accurate account – the papers will certainly tell us nothing. Stay safe Mabel and Good luck. (*Meg kisses Mabel's cheek and watches as she mounts her bike and cycles away from the crowd*)

BLACKBURN MARKET PLACE August 1917

(*Fade to applause: tomatoes splattering onto cobblestones. Feet running sound of a bicycle brake.*)

Mabel: Lydia, Mrs Hopwood – what happened to you two? What are you doing here-I thought the meeting was in the Town Hall?

Lydia: Oh, haven't you heard? Blackburn councillors have banned us from using any public meeting rooms. It's the same in nearly all the towns now. But, as you can see (*Lydia and Mrs Hopwood wipe tomatoes from their skirt and coats with their hankies*), the market lads have found a target for their rotten tomatoes – us! Before they arrived I managed to speak to a crowd though – and there was a crowd! 500 at least! I told them a thing or two. I said we women had to realise what this was war was doing to us, we've no coal, no food – we don't even know if we'll keep our jobs as weavers. I know their men are at the front, up to their necks in mud but Mrs Hopwood's son and my Earnest are in prison for not wanting to kill, and for that they put Earnest in a cell with a murderer. I said I knew their sons weren't murderers but I asked them who they thought the war was for? I said it was up to us women to get the country back to its senses and to make the government negotiate for peace. I said 'come on women – we are used to fighting for what we want' – I saw a few old faces in the crowd from the votes for women marches and when I pointed at them it made the market lads laugh. Aye and then I reminded them about how the Glasgow women got their rents fixed, and … (*Mrs Hopwood interrupts*)

Mrs Hopwood: Oh Lydia you were always such a good talker but it makes me sad to see those young lads inflamed with patriotism when we think of the terrible losses at the Somme. I'm always targeted as the mother of a Conshie in prison. The things they say about Edwin can be very distressing – if you let it get to you.

Mabel: Is there nowhere else to meet? What of the meetings planned here in September?

Mrs Hopwood: We'll manage somehow. We will NOT give in. Sylvia Pankhurst had a wonderfully successful meeting here – not that

Emmeline or Christabel would have approved. But its people like Sylvia and Mrs Despard working in the London slums who see the real misery this war is creating – not just the suffering and dying at the front but the misery and malnutrition this war inflicts on the poor. I'm going to be meeting Miss Quarmby in Oldham Mabel. They have a whole week of peace meetings planned there and a rally on the Saturday at Strawberry Gardens. I hope to see you there.

Lydia: Miss Quarmby? That's the lass they're trying to sack from her teaching post isn't it? Yes, they want no pacifist teachers spoiling their message of war do they?

Mabel: Miss Ashton has been removed from her position on the Education committee on Manchester Council too. Makes me wonder if I have a future as a teacher …

Mrs Hopwood: Do you know I read in the Daily Telegraph the Bishop of London was telling women in the slums not to reprove their children from fighting as it will stand them in good stead when it comes to hand to hand fighting with the Hun – they're telling that to the mothers of children! Mabel we'll need teachers like you when this insanity ends – don't be downhearted. We must keep the campaign going. I hear the New Zealand Field Artillery are based in Oldham – I hope they are not going to disrupt the meetings too

Mabel: Well I'd best be making tracks there since this meeting has been successfully called to a halt. Let's hope they don't disrupt any more. Hopefully I'll see you both in Oldham.

Post card to Meg

> Meeting aborted in Blackburn – off to Oldham to support the campaign there.

(Mabel stops and posts the card.)

OLDHAM: Street scene 7th August 1917: (*Riot footage Lots of Police/ New Zealand field Artillery troops*)

Mabel: (*finds Miss Quarmby collapsed against a tree*) Emma! Miss Quarmby! Goodness are you alright? (*Retrieves water bottle and hankie and wipes Emma's face*) I have been searching high and low for you. What a terrible night! Someone told me the ILP offices have been looted and our speakers had to seek refuge from the crowd in the Town Hall. They say Arthur Winterbottom was nearly killed.

Miss Quarmby: Oh Mabel! I am so pleased to see you. I have been so scared. The Anzacs think it great sport to rough up our women and attack our men. The crowd wouldn't let us speak. When the Chief Constable cancelled the meeting the speakers left, but the soldiers and the crowd followed them. Wilfred and the others have been badly hurt – it looks like our Peace mission is cancelled – and all before we uttered a word.

Mabel: What happened to you?

Miss Quarmby: I was making my way back after the riot and was followed by the New Zealanders. I think they thought I was Miss Ashton at first – they would never dare touch her. Then when I tried to speak about peace they tore my hat off and flung me round before leaving me here. (*Mabel shows concern. Miss*

Quarmby dries her eyes) They under-estimate my resolve. I am writing to the *Oldham Chronicle* about this! These men owe a courtesy to the town that's hosting them. It seems they have lost any sense of the fair play you should expect from soldiers.

Mabel: I think they were told we were proposing a surrender, rather than a negotiated peace. I will write to the paper too. But what about you? Is it true the education committee here in Oldham are threatening to sack you?

Miss Quarmby: Yes it seems I'm due to follow the proud precedent of Miss Ashton – how can they treat her like that after all she has done for the women and children of Manchester? One day Mabel, one day soon I hope, people will see this war cannot continue. We can't fight our way to the negotiating table. Maybe then our 'white feather crew' will be given the tolerance and understanding they deserve.

Mabel: You humble me with your resolve Emma. (*Fades*)

Post card to Meg from Mabel

We have faced considerable violence in Oldham. Our speakers have been attacked by the Anzacs with support from the crowd. All meetings have been cancelled by Mr Hill. Emma Quarmby and I are writing to the *Oldham Chronicle* in protest at the violence.

(*Posts the card*)

NELSON Aug 1917

15,000 on Demo

(*Marchers are seen gathering walking through Nelson past Nancy Shimbles house. We see a marcher knocking on a door and talking to a woman, then handing her a poster. The woman shuts the door and then you see her fixing the poster in her window. We see the marchers walking on….Fade*

The choir come into view holding placards and banners and singing Bread and Roses)

Mrs Ingham: Women of Nelson – look at you all! Welcome to Clarion House. Let's give a big hand to Mrs Cooper who spoke to you earlier in Victoria Park and to the Clarion singers.

We are here today to remember our comrade Miss Shimbles (*huge cheer*). Let us pledge to work hard in her memory comrades. She knew that we have to speak out against the slaughter, she knew that women understand how war affects us all, men women and children. Let us work for peace (*huge cheer*) Let us work against the capitalist military machine. Who benefits from this war? Shall we bring Germany to her knees by punishing her women and children? Read our leaflet – read *The Leader* – look we're selling it here – only 1d.

There is death in our streets, death in our families and your men are fighting – for what? A war brought on by secret diplomacy, a war brought on by the capitalists selling guns, selling bombs and making money from our food! And the men HAVE to fight! My boys are in prison – like lots of our comrades from the ILP (*huge cheer*) so women it is down to us now. We must argue for peace, we must persuade the government to negotiate. Look at us here – are we not strong? Women we know what this is doing to us – our sons, husbands, slaughtered, our freedom of speech stopped. We are harassed at every turn by the government and the wretched Defence of the Realm Act! Our leaflets are seized; the ILP raided all over the country, men who stand up for conscience flung into prison.

Women it is time to act. We are the ones who can change all this – women of Nelson – great is your power. Use it in the name of reason and humanity.

(Rival demo of drunken soldiers: Shouts of Cowards, traitors
An older woman in a shawl pushes through the crowd)

Woman: Let me speak to them. LET ME SPEAK!

Voice in the crowd: Let her speak! *(She is helped up onto the wagon, the hubbub dies)*

Woman: Listen! I speak to you as a mother. This time last year I was the mother of 3 strapping sons- all called up like you – all thinking they were doing their bit. Today I have one son. In two days I lost two boys at the Somme. Teddy and Arthur. Mown down, buried somewhere in the mud, far from home, far from everything they hold dear. And what was their sacrifice for? I tell you, they never had a chance! I know some of what they endured from my youngest – he survived and wishes he had not. He's a young lad of 18 but his lungs have been nigh on destroyed by mustard gas. He is blind. Part of his jaw has been blown away and he is wasting away, disfigured, unable to eat anything but liquid food. Worse he cannot sleep, he still relives the hell they sent him too every day. He has begged me many times to put him out of his misery. And what has the government done for him? They have yet to give him the pittance of a pension and we rely on charity to stay alive. This war has robbed me of any grandchildren I might have had, it has robbed my sons of a life. (*Muted opposition*)

Listen to me! I do not want any more lads killed. I do not want any more mothers' hearts broken. This war could end tomorrow if the government took action now to end it. There will be scars on my heart forever. These Peace campaigners are no cowards – they speak the truth! Listen to them. And if you won't listen to them take it from one of your one Jim Simmons – the lad who lost his foot at the front. He has talked all over the country about the need for peace. He's even been arrested for telling folk the real truth – you try heckling him! (*A stunned silence*)

Mrs Swanwick: I want to thank the last speaker. Could she have described the losses of war more eloquently or the brave soldiers like Private Simmons who are risking arrest campaigning for peace? You will be pleased to know Ellen Wilkinson is even now challenging his arrest at Rochdale. I would also like to commend the Bradford Pioneer for publishing the Declaration to the Government of our eminent poet Siegfried Sassoon. He is a war hero, yet he believes this war is evil and unjust. We must remember anguish unites us with the women of Austria and Germany. We are sharing the same pain and grief over our losses. Listen! We are not asking for a peace at any price – we are asking for a lasting honourable peace that will stand the test of time. We do not want our 'honour' protected by the lifeblood of our boys. We want a future where men and women can stand together in a country where there is a just and lasting peace, where our children can grow up without fear, where we unite across the world in peace and harmony. I see some of the league women here – take courage - this war cannot go on much longer the mood is changing. Things will be different when we get the vote. Six million women might have the chance to register – we have the chance to change the world when we get the vote and stop this criminal waste of human life.

Mabel: Ah! Changing the world! There's a thought – perhaps I will go into politics when we get the vote and we women can build a better future. Look at Miss Ashton and Mrs Swanwick, as clever and sharp as any man. People will not forget women like them – with the courage and determination to work for a world free from the brutality and consequences of war. That is something to strive for – however long it takes.

Illustration by Emily Johns

Making the film: October 1st, 2016

Photographs courtesy of Charlotte Bill

Suggestions for further reading:

Johanna Alberti, *Beyond suffrage: feminists in war and peace, 1914-28,* Macmillan, London, 1989.

Sarah Boston, *Women workers and the trade union movement,* Davis-Poynter, London, 1980.

Gertrude Bussey and Margaret Tims, *Pioneers for peace, Women's International League for peace and Freedom 1915-1965,* George Allen and Unwin, London, 1965.

Mary Davis, *Sylvia Pankhurst: a life in radical politics,* Pluto, London, 1999.

June Hannam and Karen Hunt, *Socialist women: Britain, 1880s to 1920s,* Routledge, London, 2002.

June Hannam, *Isabella Ford 1855-1924,* Blackwell, Oxford, 1989.

James Hinton, *Protests and visions: peace politics in 20th-Century Britain,* Hutchinson, London, 1989.

Sandra Stanley Holton, *Suffrage days: stories from the women's suffrage movement in Britain, 1865-1918,* Routledge, London, 1996.

Angela V. John, *Evelyn Sharp: rebel woman 1869-1955,* Manchester University Press, Manchester, 2009.

Angela V. John, *War, Journalism and the Shaping of the Twentieth century: the life and times of Henry W. Nevinson,* I.B. Taurus, London, 2006.

Walter Kendall, *The Revolutionary Movement in Britain 1900-1921,* Wiedenfield and Nicolson, London, 1969.

Thomas C. Kennedy, *The hound of conscience: a history of the No-Conscription Fellowship, 1914-1919,* University of Arkansas Press, Fayetteville, 1981.

Jill Liddington, *The Long Road to Greenham Common: feminism and anti-militarism in Britain since 1820*, Virago, London, 1991.

Jill Liddington, *Rebel Girls*, Virago, London, 2006.

Jill Liddington, *The life and times of a respectable rebel: Selina Cooper 1864-1946*, Virago, London, 1984.

Jill Liddington and Jill Norris, *One hand tied behind us: the rise of the women's suffrage movement*, Rivers Oram, London, 2000.

Ronan, Alison, *'A small vital flame' Anti-war women' networks in the North West of England 1914-1918,* Scholars Press 2010

Ronan, Alison, *Unpopular Resistance: The Rebel Networks of Men and Women in Opposition to the First World War in Manchester and Salford 1914 – 1918*. North West Labour History Society 2015.

Marvin Swartz, *The Union of Democratic Control in British politics during the First World War*, Clarendon Press, Oxford, 1971.

Dorothy Thompson, *Over our dead bodies: women against the bomb*, Virago, London, 1983.

Jo Vellacott, Pacifists, *patriots and the vote: the erosion of democratic suffragism in Britain during the First World War*, Palgrave Macmillan, Basingstoke, 2007.

Jo Vellacott, *From Liberal to Labour with women's suffrage: the story of Catherine Marshall*, McGill-Queen's University Press, Montreal, 1993.

Betty D. Vernon, *Ellen Wilkinson 1891-1947*, Croom Helm, London, 1982.

Bernard Waites, *A class society at War: England 1914-1918*, Berg, Leamington Spa, 1988.

Women and peace: the struggle continues – today's Crusading Women *by Jane Ward, Lizzie Gent and Jenni Gomes*

The 1914-18 war was not 'the war to end all wars.'

Today around 40 armed conflicts rage across the world, with many countries involved as combatants, financiers or arms suppliers. The number of people killed in armed conflict in 2015 was the highest for 25 years and 60 million people, more than the population of South Africa, have been forced to flee their homes. As the costs and consequences of war escalate, peace is needed more than ever so women across the world are still organising with other women to challenge the male dominated politics of war.

Women need peace. We bear huge hardships in war. We are killed and injured, we cope with the pain of bereavement, and we become heads of households when men disappear to fight. Women and children are forced to flee their homes because of war and we become targets of repression, kidnap, rape and sexual assault; over 200,000 women have been raped in ten years of war in the Democratic Republic of Congo.

Yet women refuse to be victims. We work to keep our families and communities strong and healthy. Courageous Syrian women in besieged areas take massive risks to help smuggle medicine or food past checkpoints, creating vital supply lines that people need to survive. Other women have founded civil society organisations which respond to the need for local peace and democracy-building, humanitarian assistance, and psycho-social support.

We have never stopped working for peace. After WW1 the *Cooperative Women's Guild* carried on campaigning for peace and many other matters important to women until it closed in June 2016 after 133 years. *The Women's International League for Peace and Freedom* was founded in 1915 arising directly from the women's peace conference at The Hague which brought together 1200 women from all over the world including Germany and Austria. WILPF is still active today with seven local branches, and campaigns on disarmament, human rights, women peace and security, environment and militarism. They recently launched a campaign to 'Move the Money' from military spending to fund women, peace and security initiatives.

The *Greenham Common women's peace camp* was established at RAF Greenham Common in Berkshire in September 1981 after a Welsh group, Women for Life on Earth, arrived at Greenham to protest against the decision of the British government to allow cruise missiles to be based there. It continued in various forms until 2000, and at its height over 50,000 women encircled the base in December 1982. The Manchester Greenham Support Group of local women worked tirelessly during the 1980s, transporting women to and from the camp, sending food and other essential supplies, running benefits to fundraise and even recording Greenham songs.

The Nobel Peace prize has recognised women's vital role in peace. Betty Williams and Mairead Corrigan were jointly awarded the Nobel Peace Prize in 1976 to honour their work in co-founding the Community of Peace People, an organisation dedicated to promoting a peaceful resolution to the Northern Ireland conflict. Tawakkul Karman is a journalist and peace and pro-democracy activist in Yemen who founded the group *Women Journalists Without Chains* which reports on human rights violations during war. She was jointly awarded the 2011 Nobel Peace Prize, with the Liberian president, Ellen Johnson Sirleaf, and Leymah Gbowee, a Liberian peace campaigner.

In 2016 women are still agitating for peace. We are active on the front line as Syrian women journalists risk their lives to report truth from the battlefield. We are demanding a voice in peace building across the world to make sure that women's needs are not ignored. Manchester women are still working for peace in local, national and international women only and mixed groups. We are also involved with amazing women's organisations supporting and campaigning with refugees and people seeking asylum as a direct result of war such as Women Asylum Seekers Together (WAST), the Lesbian Immigration Support Group and Safety4Sisters North West.

The Peace Garden at the top of St Peter's Square was developed to celebrate Manchester's role as a 'City of Peace' in 1986. Barbara Pearson's "Messenger of Peace" sculpture was unveiled in April 1986 and the Garden also included several memorials. The City Council removed the Peace Garden in 2013 to redevelop St Peter's Square and Friends of Manchester Peace Garden quickly formed to campaign for a new site and to promote the need for somewhere in the city for peace and quiet contemplation. They also made links with other local groups including the Manchester branch of No Glory in War. This group has run two day schools highlighting the different, hidden and untold stories of World War One as a counterbalance to the jingoistic slant of the 100 year commemorative events.

In a similar vein, an exhibition about conscientious objectors, originally developed for the Friends Meeting House, was displayed at Alexandra Park Lodge, and on heritage open day in September 2016. Visitors made "a peace tree" and collected messages on cardboard doves which were hung on the tree. Messages included "remember the past..live in the present..look forward to the future"; "we pray for peace in places of conflict including Iraq, Syria, Israel and Palestine". The Exhibition helped to focus on the issues of war and peace then and now.

Inspirational organisations working across the world for peace.

Friends of Manchester Peace Garden
https://www.facebook.com/FriendsofManchesterPeaceGroup

Greater Manchester CND is part of the national campaign to ban nuclear weapons. It co-ordinates local, regional and specialist CND groups in Greater Manchester
www.gmdcnd.org.uk.
https://gmdcnd.com

Rethink Rebuild Society – The Voice of the Syrian Community of Manchester strives to promote and raise awareness of Syrian issues within the British landscape through work on policy and media.
www.rrsoc.org (Syrian organisation in Manchester)

Greater Manchester Stop the War Coalition opposes British foreign warmongering policies, sanctions & military attacks on Iran, support Palestinian rights, https://www.facebook.com/Greater-Manchester-Stop-the-War-Coalition-262524980601747

Aldermaston Women's Peace Camp is held on the second full weekend of each month to protest against the UK's nuclear weapons.
www.aldermaston.net

Menwith Hill Women's Peace Camp holds a weekly vigil
email info@yorkshirecnd.org.uk

Faslane Peace Camp was set up near the base in 1982 and has been occupied since then.
http://faslanepeacecamp.wordpress.com

Women's International League for Peace and Freedom UK
www.wilpf.org.uk

The International Women's Peace Group aims to achieve world peace
http://internationalwomenspeacegroup.org

Women in Black started holding vigils in Jerusalem in January 1988, in response to the beginning of the first Palestinian Intifada. Women wearing black stood together in silent vigil every Friday with the message Stop the Occupation, and vigils continue today.
www.womeninblack.org

Campaign Against the Arms Trade (CAAT) is a UK-based organisation working to end the international arms trade.
https://www.caat.org.uk

International Campaign to Abolish Nuclear Weapons (ICAN) is a global campaign coalition working to mobilise people in all countries to inspire, persuade and pressure their governments to initiate and support negotiations for a treaty banning nuclear weapons.
www.ican.org

Mines Action Group (MAG) focuses on helping people to be safe from landmines and unexploded ordnance (UXO), free from danger, free from fear.
www.maginternational.org

Peace Direct is an international charity dedicated to supporting local peace builders who work at great personal risk on crucial problems like child soldiers, women and conflict, youth and peace, political violence.
www.peacedirect.org

Peace Pledge Union has been campaigning against war since 1934.
www.ppu.org.uk

Peace News is a magazine focusing on peace issues and nonviolent social change
http://peacenews.info

Who's who in the Project

Researchers on Crusading Women project

Alexandra Park – **Jenni Riley, Jenni Gomes** and **Angela Downing**

Manchester – **Jane Ward, Lizzie Gent** and **Cordelia Kuster**

Oldham – **Sheila Goodyear** and **Dorothy Bintley**

Bolton – **Lois Dean, Barry Mills** and **Margaret Koppens**

Blackburn – **Hayley Wells**

Nelson and Burnley – **Denise North** and **Sue Nike**

Rochdale – **Pete Gascoigne**

Bradford – **Eve Haskins**

Cumbria – **Hilary Chuter**

Local archivists

Mary Painter from Blackburn, **Roger Ivens** from Oldham, **Julie Lamara** from Bolton, **Sarah Hobbs** and **Dylan Lawson** from Archives+

Actors

Mabel Phythian – **Florence King**

Meg Tout – **Eve Francis**

Margaret Ashton – **Lydia Meryll**

Eva Gore Booth – **Claire Cowell**

Lydia Leach – **Emma Thomas**

Mary Hopwood – **Pam Stother**

Charlotte Despard – **Val Collier**

Emma Quarmby – **Emma Elliot**

Gertrude Ingham – **Linda Carter**

Woman In crowd – **Hazel Roy**

Helena Swanwick – **Caroline Melliar Smith**

Soldier – **Geoff Westby**

Weaver – **Alison Ronan**

Open Voice choir

Costume adviser – **Lindsay Holmes**

Nelson Co-ordinator – **Sue Nike**

Crew: **Nick Gordon-Smith, Mick Duffield, Steve Stevenson.**

Research co-ordinator **Alison Ronan**

Script writer **Hazel Roy**

Film maker **Charlotte Bill.**

Examples of the WPC handbills
(John Rylands Library)

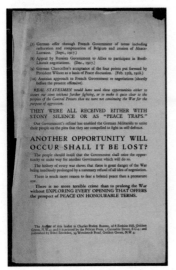

Anonymous writer: Women's
International League newsletter 1917

*I never go out without a bundle of peace
negotiation and anti-conscription leaflets,
folded so that the title is clearly seen, and
I give out as I go on my ordinary way, to
motor bus conductors, postmen, taxi-drivers,
dust collectors, gas company employees and
any men who belong to the higher ranks
of labour. I give away dozens of these a
day and never receive anything but smiles
of recognition: the men either read the
leaflet straightaway or put them quietly
in their pockets. When possible I have a
little talk about the petition. Two dustmen
have taken forms to get filled – one bus
conductor promised to talk to 'the men in
his yard.' Yesterday when I was canvassing
two men in an omnibus, a third man bent
across and asked for a leaflet. Another easy
form of propaganda is to guarantee the
sale of pacifist papers at newspaper shops. I
guarantee the sale of the Labour Leader and
the Herald at three small shops in Chelsea
and one in the country. Any remaining copies
I buy and send to middle class and working
people I hear of in the country and seaside.
In many cases I know the papers are shared.*

1918: and beyond.

The Crusade continued throughout the North West during1918, with more branches being established every week. In February 1918, the organising committee estimated 100 branches including Plymouth, Penzance, Okehampton, Swindon, Derby, Wakefield, Reading, Hull and Nottingham. Crusaders picketed the model of the warship Dreadnought in Birmingham – handing out disarmament leaflets. Members of the Crusade and the Workers' Suffrage Federation had stormed the House of Commons at least once, with peace banners and leaflets. By May 1918 Nora Hague had become the national organiser and by September 1918 there were 123 branches, at least 2 with over 1000 members.

During 1917-1918, he *Labour Leader* noted a new rush of imprisonments under new DORA regulations. The WPC took up the Lansdowne "memorial", a petition established after the publication of the Lansdowne letter written by Lord Lansdowne to the *Daily Telegraph* in late November 1917, asking for a revision of war aims in order to hasten a negotiated peace. Burnley WPC ordered 5000 sheets of the memorial, while Birmingham WPC ordered 4000. Other cities too collected signatures.

In Parliament the House was divided three times in 1917 over debates about the possibilities of 'peace by negotiation'. But this persistent effort to raise the issue of a negotiated peace in Parliament gave another edge to the WPC. Their leaflets delivered to working-class communities during 1917 echoed Lansdowne's position and asked women on the door step, '*[can] we can get our just aims without fighting to the bitter end?*'

By October 1918, there were over 40,000 signatures on the memorial.

The column in the *Leader* continued until the end of the war, regular meetings happened throughout the North West with women still travelling to support local Crusades. Ethel Snowden visited Blackburn, Burnley and Bolton in October 1918.

Once peace was declared in November 1918, many Crusaders turned their energies to contesting a general election, thinking about post war reconstruction, releasing conscientious objectors still in prison and working for Fight the Famine organisations set up in 1918 to relieve hunger in Russia and the defeated countries.

The determination of the women crusaders in East Lancashire in 1917-18 still echoes down the years in contemporary campaigns for international peace and social justice. The 'ordinary' crusader is not forgotten.

Crusading Women 2016 Photo courtesy Charlotte Bill

Women in 1915 after the International Congress of Women at The Hague